AF255442

Guided Meditations For Deep Sleep: 10 Hours Of Positive Affirmations, Hypnosis& Breathwork-Relaxation, Self-Love & Overcoming Anxiety, Overthinking, Insomnia& Depression

By
Self-healing Mindfulness Academy

Table Of Contents

Guided Meditation for Overcoming Anxiety

Welcome to this guided meditation for overcoming anxiety. This will provide you the ability to free yourself from worries and stress. Practise this session whenever you like, but preferably a time you know you won't be distrubed for 30 minutes or so. Simply find a quiet and comfortable spot. Get yourself into a comfortable position. I would recommend lying on your back, with your hands relaxed by your sides, with your legs relaxed, straight and slightly opened to the ceiling.

Now you are comfortable position, shift you to focus to my voice and simply follow my guidance. As you follow along, this meditation will guide you, helping you release any anxiety, feel relief, and find your place of peace within.

Prepare your body and mind for this meditation, for relaxation. Allow yourself to embrace and enjoy the peace this session provides you, simply from the release of all your anxiety and disturbing thoughts. Allow your thoughts to swiftly pass through. There is no longer a need for them. There is nothing to worry over. Now, you are safe.

Take a nice, deep breath, using your stomach, so your inhale can be as deep as possible. As the air circulates through your body, bring your attention to this moment, to right now. Anxiety is usually the result of placing too much of your focus on the future, on things that haven't happened yet and may never will. As we move foward with this meditation, you will learn how to bring yourself back to this present moment. Right now, this moment is all that existsts. At this moment, all is good.

Right now, there is no better place for you do be. This time, right here, is the right thing for you and your growth. Nothing else is more of a priority than what you are doing now. There is no where else you need to be.

Reassure and trust that all will be fine. Any tension you feel will pass. You will be okay, you will reach a deep state of relaxation, and all will pass.

You deserve all the good in life, to feel great and to let go off all anxiety. Simply remain present in this moment, focusing your undivided attention. Your thoughts don't need to be protected.

Now, bring awareness to your body. Scan through your body placing your focus on each and every part and notice how they feel exactly.

Anxiety is certainly unpleasant. A mechanism to protect yourself, when really it does you more harm. You are in no danger. You are safe. There is no longer room within you to store it anymore.

Now, we will work thorugh the whole body relaxing it, part by part. Slowly work through, scanning your body, focusing on each part, and relaxing it. Notice any signs of tension, where you are holding anxiety in the body. As you come across these areas, try to relax these tense muscles. Breathe deeply allowing your breath to relax you more with every exhale.

Relax your toes and feet. Relax your ankles and legs, up to your knees, relaxing them too. Let your heavy, tight muscles, loosen and relax. Working up to your hips and glutes, relax them. Your lower half of your body is completely relaxed now. Scan it once more, noticing any areas that still cling on to any anxiety. For now, simply observe these areas and we will come back to them in a bit.

Now focus on your stomach. Bring your attention to how relaxed it feels, as it rises and falls with every breath. Then relax your chest. Allow your ribcage to move freely, simply by the air alone.

Now notice your back. How it feels against gravity or whatever surface you lay on. Imagine your spine resting neutrally in perfect alignment. As you breath now, work from the lowest point of your back upwards, gladually relaxing each section. Allow the air as you exhale to remove any tensions and anxiety. Notice any points where anxiety still clings on, and remember exactly where.

Moving up towards your hands, relax them. As your fingertips and palms face up towards the sky, allow them to release anything your holding onto, relaxing them completely. Move up your arms, relaxing your forearms, elbows and upper arms.

Now focus your attention onto your shoulders, relaxing them. Here, is an important aspect of relaxation, as often our shoulders hold most of our worries, stress and axiety. The weight of this negative energy we are not always aware of, and so remains. So, let your shoulders drop, so they rest neutrally allowing your arms to hang weightlessly from them. Release all of the weight you found yourself carrying on your shoulders. Pemit all of those concerns to leave you.

Next relax your neck, feel as the muscles loosen and your head is effortlessly held and supported. Whilst you do this, feel as your throat relaxes becoming seemingly more open. As you continue to move through your body, continue to note any spots that are still tense, making a mental note for later.

It's time to relax your head and face. So, relax the lower face area, such as your jaw and lips, making sure your tongue rests neutrally in its natural position. Let your cheeks and nose relax, allowing every last facial muscle to release and lengthen. Make sure your eyelids rest softly over your eyes and aren't being squeezed shut. Notice how good it feels to let your eyes rest. Relax your eyebrows and forehead, simply letting them rest wherevers natural. Now, relax the top of the head. Take a deep breath, feeling the whole body slip deeper into relaxation.

Now let us scan the body once more, noticing any areas that don't feel completely relaxed yet, anywhere that seems to be holding anxiety. This could be anywhere, your jaw, shoulders, back or even the forehead. Check through all parts of you, locating any anxiety that still remains.

Now, imagine these areas of tension feel hot. Visualize yourself as chocolate, something that has the ability to change state. Feel as those points grow hotter and hotter, and when warm enough, the choclate starts to melt. As your body soothingly melts, feel as your muscles become softer and more elastic, whilst any tension melts away, until they become completely relaxed and anxiety-free.

Enjoy the calming sensations you feel right now. The complete state of peace and lightness you feel, as if you are floating. This relaxation is a gift to yourself.

The most beneficial, invaluable gift, you could receive right now.

Scan the whole body once more, this time observing for where in your body feels the most relaxed. Place your focus right here, enjoying the warmth and relaxation of that part. Now, allow this sensation to spread from this area, slowly enveloping the whole body. As this relaxed zone grows, gradually saturating the body, it pushes out all anxiety.

The power of your breath will help you overcome anxiety. This is your most powerful tool, allowing you to overcome many obstacles, calming and relaxing you. So, simply focusing on your breathing is all you need to do. If your thoughts infiltrate your mind, it's okay. Don't fight them, or pass any judgement, simply put them aside. You don't need these thoughts right now.

Now, bring your focus to your breathing. Feel as the cool, refreshing air enters into your nostrils, completely filling and expanding the lungs, before leaving once more as you exhale. Simply focus on your breath alone. Place your hands on your stomach and feel how it rises and falls as the air pours in and out. Feel your lungs emptiness as the air leaves with your exhale.

Stay with your breath. If you begin to feel any anxiety arise, just take another deep breath and allow the steady rhythem of your breathing to calm you, guiding you back to this meditation.

Inhale, counting to four. One, two, three, four.

Then holding your breath, and counting to three.

One, two, three.

Exhale, counting to eight.

One, two, three, four, five, six, seven, eight.

Once more:

Inhale, counting to four.

One, two, three, four.

Hold your breath, counting to three.

One, two, three.

Exhale, counting to eight.

One, two, three, four, five, six, seven, eight.

If your mind brings thoughts distracting you, just observe it for a few moments, then let it go. Use your breath to anchor you to right now, so your focus remains with me.

Imagine the very air you inhale, contains a wonderful peaceful and calming energy, whilst the air you exhale is your anxiety. Each time you breathe out, you are letting go of tension and anxiety, leaving more room for peace and relaxation. Feel as the space for relaxation becomes bigger and bigger, whilst the space filled with anxiety shrinks, gradually becoming smaller and smaller until it exists no more. Just become aware of how your breathing soothes and calms you.

Now, as you inhale, mentally say to yourself: "Relax." Then, as you exhale, repeat "Relax."

Once again, repeat this: inhale - relax, exhale - relax.

Your body is relaxed, and your mind is calm. Your thoughts are slowing now. You are in control. You arc complctcly safc and calm.

Now, let us use this safe environment, this moment just for you, and think about how you feel when you are overwhelmed with anxiety. Understand that it is normal to feel this way when you are concerned. Whenever you next feel this way, remind yourself that it is okay and will pass.

Now, allow your mind to completely relax, too. Riht now, you don't need to focus on anything. Just enjoy this time, with the relaxation it brings you, and trust everything will be fine.

You find yourself in a special place now. A place of inner peace and tranquillity. Here there is no place for worries, no need for them. All is good. You feel relief for these calming sensations, but also, for you have learned how to get here. Just your breath and focus have brought you here. This place remains within you, and you can access it whenever you wish. Here, you will always find shelter and rest, away from your worries and anxiety.

Feel free to carry these feelings with you, even after you finish this meditation. Allow this peace to stay with you throughout your day, as you complete all you need to.

When you next feel anxiety start to take over your mind, try to remeber this meditation as this may be enough to ground you in peace. This in mind, you will be able to remain in control and release any anxiety. Simply by breathing deeply, allowing the air you take in to relax you and bring yourself to the true present moment. With your practice of this meditation, your confidence will only grow. You will know you are bigger than anything that causes your anxiety, that you can remain in control.

You are powerful. You are calm. You are free. You are peaceful. You are strong. You are hopeful. You are full of positivity. You are rejuvenated.

Now, for those of you who want to return to your day, filled with its usual tasks, when this meditation is over, it's time to wake up. So, slowly wiggle your fingers and toes and gently stretch. Whenever you feel ready, slowly open your eyes. You will take this peace with you throughout your day.

But for those of you who want to move into sleep now: continue to enjoy these feelings of relaxation allowing them to guide you into a restful sleep. Once you wake, you will feel refreshed and renewed, calm, and at peace. Sleep well, and enjoy your dreams.

Guided Meditation for Overcoming Anxiety 2

Welcome to this guided meditation for the relief of anxiety, replacing it with inner peace and balance. As you move through this meditation, you will learn how to detach yourself from any disturbing emotions enabling you to find serenity.

Now as we begin, simply prepare your body for this session. Get yourself into a comfortable position. Feel free to lie on your back or side or to sit, whatever you find most comfortable. You don't have to remain here in this position for the whole meditation, you can easily change if you find yourself in any discomfort. Only you know what is best for you.

This time is only for you. A gift to yourself. You deserve this time, simply for yourself.

Often those who suffer from anxiety, spend too much time in their head, focusing on thoughts so they are mentally absent. You may find your mind is hyperactive, chaotically busy, focused internally on your future. This means your mind doesn't give much attention to the sensations of your physical body and neglects your breathing. Perhaps your breathing rhythm is constantly short and shallow, as if you are facing real dangers constantly.

Through your practice of meditation, you will learn how to relax your body, slow your mind, and deepen your breathing, allowing you to change your current patterns in life. As you develop this skill of relaxation, your brain will understand you are safe, so it can switch off the panic button, releasing you from your anxiety.

We will also use some mantras to change your unproductive beliefs, allowing you to remove any subconscious blockages.

So follow my invitation to join me now. Simply close your eyes and follow my voice. Bring your attention to this very moment.

Now, focus on your head. Become aware of your muscles that make up your forehead and scalp, and take a moment to contract them. Then, allow them to relax. Moving down, feel any tension you hold in your eyelids, squeeze and and then relax them. Release and let go, calming and relaxing you. Relax all the muscles in the face. Then moving to your lips, tightly compress them, before letting them relax so they lay softly closed. Clench your jaw, then relax. Press your chin against your chest to tense the muscles in the back of your neck. Then slowly bring your head back up, relaxing it.

Contract your shoulder muscles, and then relax them, let them loosen allowing the shoulders to hang freely in a relaxed position.

Moving to your fists, hands and arms clench them tightly. Then release this force you hold over them, relaxing them all.

Tense the muscles in your back and then release, relaxing them, notice as they loosen, one by one, until your whole back feels lighter and relaxed. Take a deep breath in, filling your chest with air, and while you exhale, feel the muscles in your ribcage relaxing.

Pull your head and spine upwards towards the sky, feeling your abdominals tense. Then let your stomach become relaxed.

Contract your glutes, so they become firm before slowly relaxing them. Notice how you body is becoming filled with relaxation.

Finally pay attention to your leg as a whole, contracting it from the very top by your hips, to the thighs and down to the feet and toes. Then release, relaxing every part: your hips, your thighs, your knees, ankles and feet. Simply allow relaxation to take over all.

Now enjoy the sensation of complete relaxation throughout your whole body.

Moving foward, shift your focus to your breath. For now don't change a thing. Just become aware of your current cycle of breath, in and out.

Now your body is relaxed and free from any anxiety, let us use the power of your imagination to work on freeing your mind from any anxiety as well. So, visualize yourself lying on a bed of soft grass. It is a beautiful day with a clear blue sky, and the sun above soothingly warms you. Take a deep breath now and as you exhale, imagine you breathe out soap bubbles. These bubbles are filled with all your anxiety from your whole body. As you breathe out these bubbles, watch as they float away, into the sky before they pop, releasing your anxiety into the sky above.

Inhale once more, and as you do so collect all the anxiety you can find. Imagine blowing it into a bubble, just like a piece of gum and imagine blowing it into a huge bubble. Now eject this bubble, into the sky. The bubble bounces in the air upwards, far away until it finally pops out.

Repeat this process once again. Inhale deeply, expanding your stomach as you do so. Then breathe out a healthy jet of bubbles, filled with all of your anxiety. They fly all around you, glistening with the suns reflection, and taking your anxiety far from your reach. You watch as they pop and exist no more.

Now as you inhale, round up all the anxiety that still clings to you. Exhale, releasing another stream of bubbles. Watch as your worries and anxiety are now in complete control of nature, the wind slowly popping them one by one.

Now focus on the affirmations I say. Slowly repeat them to yourself, mentally or out loud, whichever you wish. Dedicate a breath to each and every one.

Inhale deeply, and repeat the mantra as you exhale.

I am aware of my breathing. I am aware of the air flowing in and out of my body.

Inhale. Exhale.

I am aware of my worries, fears and anxiety. I am aware of how they make me feel.

I'm aware of these negative thoughts and how they influence my anxiety.

I'm aware of my body's rhythem. I'm aware of the steady pace of my heart.

Between each beat, make space for the focus on your breathing alone.

Now, while I inhale and exhale, my mind slowly becomes quieter and more calm.

I am releasing all negative thoughts.

As I breath, my anxiety is calmed.

I am sinking deeper into relaxation, both my body and mind.

With every exhale, I release all my fears and worries.

With every inhale, I find yet more peace and calmness.

I inhale tranquility. I exhale anxiety.

As I'm aware of my breathing, I let go of all that doesn't serve me.

Smile as you breathe, I deserve all the best from life.

I inhale serenity. I exhale pain.

I am completely safe and grounded. I allow myself to cherish in this peace.

I am strong.

With each day, things will only get better.

I expect and am prepared for great things to come my way.

Now allow your anxiety to feel valid, tell your anxiety: I see you. I hear you. I accept you, and love you for all you are.

I allow myself to experiance all my emotions without pushing any aside. Emotions don't define me, they are just a small part of me. I can observe all emotions while reminaing calm.

Rather than rejecting and fighting against emotions, I accept them. As I do so, the load I carry around with me reduces and I feel lighter and more free. As you set them free, emotions simply flow through your body before they leave you.

Repeat to yourself , "Thank you for your help in protecting me. But I no longer need your help, as I am ready to move foward alone, liberated and free to do as I wish."

Enjoy how much more lighter and free you feel now.

I work on healing all the time, my body and mind in perfect harmony.

I grant myself this wonderful sensation of complete peace.

Now using your mind's eyes, envision you are bathing in a soothing, warm, golden light. This powerful yet gentle light healing your every part, all the way from your head to your toes. This light hugging you gently in its soft glow.

I enjoy this sensation, as if I am being wrapped in a soft, warm blanket. I feel completely safe and at peace. It's so good to feel the warm, soft glow kiss my skin.

I feel refreshed and re-energized now.

I feel wellness as it has seeped into my whole body, into each and every cell of my being.

I unwind in the comfort and peace of right here. I allow myself to absorb all this energy, revitalizing and replenishing myself with this peace.

I enjoy this moment and this completely relaxed state, free from any worries and stress.

Now, imagine you are stood at the top of a set of stairs. Picture them however you wish, winding down spirally, made of glass so you can see right below, it doesn't matter. You are simply going to move down them.

Take a deep in. As you do so count to three. One, two, three.

Now exhale, you are ready to go downstairs now, as you do so count your steps to five. One, two, three, four, five.

Pause as you inhale, counting to four. One, two, three, four.

Exhale, moving on down the stairs, counting to six now. One, two, three, four, five, six.

Pause, inhale, counting to five. One, two, three, four, five.

Exhale, moving down, counting to seven. One, two, three, four, five, six, seven.

You find yourself in a dark room now. It may be dark but you can see just enough that you know where you're going. Don't be afraid of this unknown darkness. You are safe. You are in control.

You take a few steps foward and find yourself in the centre of a room. Calmly you take a seat with your legs crossed on the cool floor. Although you can barely see, you sense an item on the floor, just infront of you. Leaning foward you pick up a small, wooden bowl.

Now, as you hold it in your hands. It's more heavy and steady than you imagined and as you run your fingers over its smooth surface you notice it is completely empty. As if waiting patiently for someone to fill it with something.

You place it gently back on the floor infront of you.

You take a moment to visualize your anxiety, a dark sand weighing down your body.

Now, you sift through your body, rounding up any sand that is lurking within you, before placing it into the bowl infront. You repeat this a few times grabbing any grains that remian inside you.

Picture your worries and stresses as icy, black stones that sit in your mind. Simarily to your anxiety, take them and place them into the bowl too. This bowl may seem small, but trust that all that has been holding you back can fit inside.

Repeat this, placing every last worry that has been bothering you, and causing your anxiety into the bowl infront. Finally, all you anxiety, stresses and negative thoughts are in the bowl.

Breathe in deeply, using your belly.

Everything is in constant movement, things constantly changing.

The dark can turn into light.

Your concerns and anxiety can change into love, peace, strength, and happiness.

Notice the bowl now. It has become much lighter and seems to glow more with your every breath. The dark sand and stones grow lighter too. The stones shining brightly like rare jewels and the sand glistening, illuminating this dark space. The bowl radiates a bright, golden light that fills the room. Now you find yourself sat in bright, clean light, absorbing it in.

Not only have your surroundings undergone change, your thoughts have too. They are no longer dark and heavy, but are shimmering, priceless jewels of luck, hope and wonderful possibilities. As you inhale, your whole body absorbs this bright, healing, empowering light. Now you glow softly, attracting more healing energy to you. You are in complete peace.

As you enjoy the wonders this room brings you, a dark thought may sneak up on you. Here you can simply direct it into the bowl infront. The bowl is here for you. The bowl can hold all the negativity you carry on your shoulders.

This room is always here, ready for you if you need to unload. So feel free to return if ever you wish.

Now, whenever you are ready, stand up, and slowly make you way back up the stairs. This time as you go upwards, take this light and jewles of positive thought with you as you go.

Now as we go upstairs, take a deep breath and count backwards with me.

Six, five, four, three, two, one.

You have arrived back where you started, although now you feel changed. You feel liberated from you worries and anxiety, which has now been replaced with peace and tranquility. Now you spread light with you as you move, and understand that whenever you need more you can return here.

Now when your ready, take a deep breath in. Exhale and slowly open your eyes. Thank you for joining me today.

Guided Meditation for Sleep

Good evening. Welcome to the meditation that will guide you into a peaceful nights sleep. All you need to do is get comfortable and focus on my voice which will lead you into a state of deep relaxation, and this can decieve even the most busy minds into a restful sleep.

You may find yourself drifting off as I speak. If this happens, don't worry. Although you may be asleep, your subconscious mind is still listening and being influenced by the positivity this meditation brings. So, you will still become relaxed on a deeper level, improving the quality of your sleep.

This day is no longer here. All you have experianced today is over, slowly drifting into your past. So now, simply give yourself to this moment. Remain present here, as there is nothing else you should be doing now. In this moment, all you shoulde be doing is enjoying the comfortable warmth of your bed. The night is here so you can rest and recover from your day, readying you for tomorrow. Your body and mind have been busy in use all day, so now is the time to give them a break and re-energize. This guided meditation will take you into a state ensuring you can rejuvenate and refresh. So now, listen to me and allow yourself to relax. Let your body take charge, relaxing at whatever pace it desires. With each breath, you can relax your body, part by part or simply as a whole.

So, simply remain present, to right here and now. Enjoy the warmth and peace this moment brings you. Feel as your pillow softly hugs your head, and the warm blanket enwraps you. Feel as your body melts into the comfort of your mattress

Now, shift your focus to your breath. Using your stomach, take a deep breath. Feel as the cool, refreshing air flows through your nostrils straight into your lungs. Then notice how this air travels back out of your body, out through your mouth. With each breath, inhale deeper and deeper. With each exhale, feel as you sinker deeper in your bed.

Smile, you are taking this time to care for yourself, to relax and recharge. Breathe in, breathe out, diving deeper into relaxation as you go. Embrace the soft touch of your bedding, how it gets more and more comfortable with each breath. As you lie here, enjoy the pleasant sensations this moment brings you. Breathe in, breath out and greet the feeling of deep relaxation.

Now feel free to imagine you are in a warm, cozy nest completely safe, or that your are peacefully floating in a boat on calm ocean waters. Whichever one you gravitate towards, you are cradled tenderly, simply listening to the water or the sounds of a gentle breeze, with your eyes resting closed.

You feel at ease, simply enjoying this moment. Breathing in, and out, you smile to yourself as you appreciate the beauty of right here. and the joy. Breathe in, breathe out, and smile to this moment and to yourself. This moment is beautiful.

Take a nice deep breath. It is time to relax the entire body now. So move your focus throughout your body, paying attention to each and every part, relaxing each. To begin, start with your toes and feet. Relax them completely before moving on up to your lower legs and knees. Feel your legs open up to the ceiling, as they accept this relaxation. Next, move up to the thighs, hips and glutes, relaxing each. Now relax your hands, starting from the fingertips, to the palms and finally the wrists. Relax your arms now too.

Bring your focus to your stomach, how it gently rises and falls with your inhale and exhale. Take another deep breath, turning your attention to your chest as you exhale. How your chest completey empties and your chest muscles become relaxed.

Now, become aware of your whole back. How are you currently holding it? Imagine now each vetebrae in perfect alignment. Observe each, starting from the base of your spine, simply relaxing each one as you move upwards, feeling just like a soothing massage. Take a deep breath in, feeling the air flow right through your spine as you exhale.

Relax your shoulders. Release all you've been carrying around with you, throughout your day. Do you have any worries? Leg them go. Are you holding any tension? If so, let it go. Are you holding onto any anger or resentment? Let that go too. As you release all negativity you have been carrying with you, feel as your shoulders become lighter and more free, now they are released of all that extra weight.

Open up your airway, relaxing the inside of your throat. Notice the back of your neck, allow it to relax supported by your soft pillow. Give your neck some relief from holding your head up all day. It deserves this time now, simply for rest.

Pay attention to your head now, granting it this relaxation. Yours ears work constantly, even through the night, so give them all the relaxation they need. Notice how you are holding your jaw. Let your jaw release. All you need to focus on is your body moving deeper into relaxation. So, relax the tongue, lips and cheeks, allowing them to rest without tension. Move to your forehead and eyebrows, making sure they are holding no tension and simply becoming more relaxed. Lastly let your eyelids lay calmly over your tired eyes. They deserve a good rest right now as well, so enjoy the sensation as they sink further into your head.

Finally, let us focus on the body as a whole. Give the very surface of the body the opportunity to relax. Visualize your skin and relax it too, for it needs to recharge and rejuvenate as well. Now imagine the inside of your body. Observe all your organs that work for you all the time. Mentally send them your love and care, allowing them to relax.

Moving foward its time to work on relaxing your mind now. Give yourself permission to let go of any emotions that crowd your mind. Release all sadness, anger, jealousy, any fears or worries- just let them go. These emotions are valid, so don't be hard on yourself. You deserve your own forgiveness for any of your mistakes, so just let go. Overthinking or holding that grudge is only slowing your progress, so forgive yourself and let go. Accept any of these emotions, they are simply part of the learning process.

Your mind is likely busy with thoughts, running through chaotically. Try your best to let them pass through you. It is expected that thoughts and pictures may cross your mind as your trying to relax. Just observe them, setting them aside for another time. Now, these thoughts are not needed. Right here, you have nothing to do. There is no task, or anything for you to accomplish. The night is here, simply for your productive rest. The best thing you can do right now is allow your body this time for a rewarding recharge.

Now, imagine your mind operating just like a spinning wheel. Spinning round quickly at the pace of your thoughts. Visualize this wheel and its speed, how it gradually slows. It continues to gently slow, until finally it reaches a stop. Your mind now calm, clear as it has slipped into a deep state of relaxation. Now, ready to move into it's dreamy state.

Take a deep breath, as you exhale, let go of all you don't need, all you don't love and all that holds you back. As this negativity is released and your mind more clear, allow the inner light and clarity to spread throughout your body.

If your mind brings up any thoughts or emotions, continue to let them pass through, without your engagement. Stay calm. Stay present. Simply remain in this moment, as you slip further into relaxation.

Focus on your breathing without the urge to change anything. Observe its deep steady rhythm as you enjoy feeling cozy, at peace, in a warm nest or floating calmly in a boat.Do nothing but simply enjoying this moment.

Inhale deeply. Then exhale, feeling again how your body relaxes on a deeper level. All you carry that you dont need, fades away. You are carefree. Now all you feel is calm, peace and easiness.

Inhale, Exhale.

Right now, you have all the time in the world for just you. There is no where to rush to. Everything you could possibly need is right with you. You are in the right place, where everything happens as you need. Time is of no limit now. All is good.

Hand over all your worries and stresses. Leave everything to a higher power, and trust that all will be well and fall into place perfectly.

Allow your inner smile to be released, smiling to yourself and life.

Feel as you are liberated from your worries. Embracing the serenity and carefreeness of here, finding nothing but harmony in this moment.

Breathe in, breathe out. Feel a soothing comfort, just like your body and your mind are visiting a mental spa.

Drift deeper now, into sleep. Trust that all is well, and allowing yourself into this dreamy state.

Sleep well, and enjoy your sweet dreams.

Guided Meditation for Deep Sleep 2

Good evening. Welcome to this meditation, which will prepare you for a restful nights sleep. So, let's get started straight away by making yourself comfortable in wherever you plan to sleep. Make yourself as warm and comfortable as you can. All you need to do is let my voice guide you, although don't stress if you find yourself asleep before I finish. Sometimes sleep comes fast and easily, whereas other times it seems to never come. It's okay if you don't slip into sleep during the meditation. Either way, your body and mind will enjoy this time to rest and relax, exactly the same as if you were asleep.

Simply allow yourself to remian present in this exact moment. This time, is simply for rest, so you can recover from your day. Relish the comfort your bed provides you with. You you sink into your pillows and mattress, fully supported. Feel the peace and warmth of right here. You are thankful your day has passed and appreciate all the good this day brought you. But for now, it is time to let go, allow this day to enter your past, so you can stay entirely in the present.

Shift your focus to your breath. Inhale slowly and deeply, noticing how the air flows through your body and back out again as you exhale. Sense any tense parts of your body. For now, this is the time for your complete relaxation. As you exhale, feel the top of your head start to relax. Breathe in, and breathe out, relaxing your cheeks and jaw now. With your next breath, turn you attention to your mouth, noticing as this cool, refreshing air relaxes your throat. Inhale. Exhale, relaxing your lips, tongue and cheeks. Notice any tension you are holding in your forehead and eyebrows. Breathe in, before breathing them all out, letting them relax. With your next breath relax your eyelids, allowing them to rest calmly over your eyes. Exhale, relaxing your whole head once again.

Take a deep breath, becoming aware of how you are holding your neck. Exhale, relaxing all the muscles there. Relax the front, sides and back allowing your pillow to fully support your head. Your neck has done all it needs today. Now, all it needs is rest.

Inhale using your stomach, and exhale feeling your shoulders drop and relax. Release all the weight you've been carrying through the day, let it be swept up by your breath.

Breathe in, allowing your lungs to be filled with air. Breathe out, letting your chest deflate and drop down, completely relaxed.

Inhale again, filling the stomach with air. Exhale, letting your stomach sink, relaxing completely.

Now as you breathe in, notice how the muscles of your back feel. Exhale, relaxing all the muscles in your lower back. Take another breath in and exhale, this time relaxing all the muscles in your upper back. Breath in, devoting this breath to your back as a whole. Visualize how all the tesnion from your back is released through your spine.

Now moving on, pay attention to all the tension you're holding in your around your hip level. Exhale, releasing all. Relax your hips. Relax all that's here on your body.

Breathe in, and feel as the air begins to target the tension in your legs.

Exhale, allowing your glutes, thighs and calves to relax.

Inhale. Exhale, and feel your entire legs relax. As they do so, let them drift open and face up to the ceiling. Allow your ankles and feet this relaxation. Relax your toes. Take a deep breath, and exhale noticing your entire legs are now completely relaxed.

Inhale deeply, notice any tension that remains within you, let it all go with your exhale.

Now, imagine you find yourself on a mountain in a beautiful, enchanting forest. The late afternoon sun beams through the leaves overhead, glistening in spots every few steps. You have had a tiring day, walking through nature. Notice how the green leaves of the trees sway gently in the breeze, as you make your way down the small, winding narrow path. The birds make a peaceful, calming song whilst the whole forest listens, appreciating its beauty. You are tired.

Your legs lazily continue on this pathway. They need rest.

You move downhill, carried by its push rather than your own legs. Whilst you are here your mind keeps drifting to the thought of a cozy pillow and soft blanket. You feel sleepiness take over, and you begin to yawn.

This day is nearly over, the sun looking to retire from yet another day. The evening is closing in. The birds sing their gentle song, preparing to settle in their warm nests for the night. You would love to lay down right here, soothed by the forest. But you have to keep moving foward, down and round, so you can make it to the cottage before the sun goes down, placing the forest into darkness. The path leads you straight to the cottage, straight to sleep. As you move the forest is peaceful. The gentle sounds of this place- the soft rustle of the leaves and grass, the relaxing birds song and even the sound of your steps as you move foward, makes you more and more sleepy.

You move steadily down the path, wishing you will reach the cottage soon. Your legs are tired and all you seek is to sink into your warm, comfortable bed and rest.

Now take a deep breath in, and start to count each step you make down this path and through the forest. Inhale, counting to four. Exhale, counting your steps down the path: one, two, three, four, five, six.

You are yawing now, ready for the comfort of your bed. Inhale again, counting to four: one, two, three, four. Exhale, counting your steps down the path: one, two, three, four, five, six. Evening has arrived. The forest becomes slowly darker and darker. The sounds of the forest begin to settle, becoming quiet. As if it is now time for nature to sleep. There is no longer beams of sunlight shining through the trees, but instead the soft glow of the moon and stars in the dark sky. You are so close to the cottage now, just a few more steps. Your legs feel heavy and your body is about to fall asleep. Your mind is calm and clear, soothed by the enchanting forest.

You are here now. You open the door of the warm cottage. Take a nice, slow, deep breath. As you exhale, count. One, two, three, four, five, six. You are so sleeping now counting is difficult. Inhale. Exhale. One, two, three, four, five, six. You are finally at your bed now. You lay down, your body sinking into the cozy mattress and pillows. Your bed soothes your tired body. It is time to sleep now.

Your feet are sleeping. Your heavy leg muscles gently falling asleep too. You relax allowing yourself to fall into sleep. Your back muscles soften and are sleeping. Your head is relaxed and sleeping. Your eyes, gently covered by your eyelids are sleeping. Your body is falling asleep, part by part. Finally, your whole body is sleeping now. Your mind asleep and emotion free. Goodnight.

Guided Meditation for Self-healing

Welcome to the meditation for self-healing. Whether you don't feel well, have or are looking for a diagnosis, or suffer from chronic pain, this meditation is for you. This will help you use your body's ability to heal itself. During this meditation, I will guide you into a deeply relaxed state. From this state, you will then have the opportunity to truely talk to your body, sending it love and empowering it to heal.

To maximize your self-healing, practice this meditation as often as possible. You can heal no matter the time of day. So even if you fall asleep during, your sunconscious is still following along with the meditation, aiding your body in its self-healing.

So to begin, get yourself into a comfortable position. You should be pleasantly warm, so no discomfort can disrupt the session. Allow yourself this time to simply relax. Place your hand over your heart, feel its beat and allow it to guide you into relaxation. As your body begins to relax, notice how it begins to soften.

Now, imagine a warm, golden light spread through your body. It infiltrates through your muscle tissues sinking right into your bones. This golden light, travels up through your feet, to your lower legs, knees, moving gradually up your thighs and hips. It doesn't stop here; it moves through to your stomach before slowly encompassing your entire body. Feel as this warm, soothing light spreads through your hands, arms, shoulders, neck and back. Enjoy the relaxing sensation it brings. Right now, the best thing you could be doing is bathing in this golden, healing light. Knowing just this, continue to allow relaxation to seep in, until your whole body is completely relaxed and you feel as if you are floating. Your whole body is filled with the bright, golden light. This light has coated every organ, every system, radiating in all directions, and shining out through your skin.

The negativity, all toxins and unproductive emotions you carry hide in the darkness within you. This light you are now illuminated with transforms any areas of darkness, placing it into light and therefore relieving you of the weight you carry on your shoulders. Now all your negative thoughts, doubts and concerns no longer have a place to reside inside of you. There is no longer a place for anger, jealousy and hatred to hide, no corner to linger anymore.

Now, imagine you are taking a walk through nature, on a warm summers evening. The air is a perfect, cool temperature. Around you you hear the chirp of the crickets in the grass, and the soothing sound of the bird's song overhead. You walk down a small, narrow path, trees and flowers growing alongside, gently swaying in the breeze. The path flows away, carrying you with it.

As you've been carried down this path, you now find yourself stood before a large tree. This tree may be old, but strong and healthy, it offers large branches as a home for many. Birds, squirrels and insects enjoy calling this tree home, whilst most animals enjoy some relief from the sun on hot, summers days by sitting underneath it. This tree towers over all others near, whilst its roots spread deep into the ground, connecting to the source of life. Take a step forward and place your hand on the tree trunk infront of you. Imagine you are absorbing some of this trees mighty life power. Feel yourself connect with this higher intelligence, this tree has been able to absorb from touching the sky. Notice as you become more and more grounded, just like the deep roots of this tree. Feel as the powerful, green energy flows through you, right from the top of your head, down to the tips of the toes.

Now you find yourself sat down under the tree. Leaning up against the tree, you listen to the sounds of nature. The green wood behind you fully supports you, allowing you to shift your focus to your body. Take a deep breath and simply appreciate your body for all it does for you every single day. Think about every last way it supports you, even when you are at rest. You are thankful for this higher intelligence that works within your body, beating your heart and pumping blood through your veins. Digesting your food and nourishing your every cell and managing all systems within you. It protects you from the outer world and holding your wonderful soul. Take this moment to appreciate all that, consciously telling your body "I Love you". The world works by responding to the vibration of love, plants, animals even water responds to love. Your body is not an exception. So feel as your body responds to these words, to this love and affection.

Now, thank your legs for carrying you, on your journey through this beautiful world. Thank your hands for serving you for so long already. Thank your back for holding you straight and supporting you. Thank your neck for holding your head, assisting in every precious movement of your head. Thank you stomach and digestive system, for digesting all the food you eat. You feel truly blessed, you are able to move, run, jump and trust that your body does all it needs for you. Thank your brain, for being with you at all times, assisting you in all ways and simply being a powerful central. Thank your mouth enabling you to express yourself, feel tastes, laugh and kiss. Thank your nose for helping you breathe and notice wonderful scents. Thank you eyes for providing you with vision, so you can see amazing things. Just let all this gratefulness sink in.

Now, repeat these words I say, mentally or out loud: Body, I love you. I accept and appreciate all of you. I know you perform as best you can. I wish you great health. You deserve the best, so you can function perfectly. I enwrap you in my love, for you are amazing. My love seeps into every organ, every tissue, and every bone. My love circulates through every system and every cell because I truly love all they do for me. I give you my blessing, so energy and good health can flow through me.

I trust you. I trust in your ability to heal yourself. So, I invite your wisdom and power to do as you know best, for you.

Take a few deep, purposeful breaths. Then allow the air from your breath to flow through you as it normally would. Allow the healing power of your breath to settle throughout your body. Feel as this infinite love and gratitude spreads through you now. You have all you need to heal.

Allow these wonderful sensations to remain within you. Feel as these sensations of love, purity and calmness spreads, softening and warming you, starting right from your heart. Feel unconditional and eternal love. Feel completely grounded and complete. Enjoy this sensation. Let this feeling spread from your heart, slowly growing throughout your entire being. Simply let your body soak it all up.

Now, observe how your body feels, noticing any area of your body that may need some extra love and care. Pour love into that part in particular, which may need some more help in healing. Imagine a warm, golden, healing light pours into that part, overwhelming it with its shining power. This part of you is bathed in light, removing all its issues and pain that usually settles in the darkness here. This light brings perfect balance and harmony, giving this part the special attention it requires. This light heals and soothes not only this part but your whole body. It restores a perfect equilibrium, so your body has the perfect conditions is needs, as if you've been reborn! Your body deserves to work at its best, and absolure health is the best natural condition to allow this. You are created to be unique, complex and absolutely healthy. Only your body knows just how to restore all functions and cure itself.

Enjoy the peacefulness of this moment. Feel how your body responds to this wonderful, relaxed state. Your body is thankful for this opportunity you have given to it. It is grateful for this time and care but also the trust you have placed in it. Right here, is the best place for your body to be. A safe space full of peace, calmness, serenity, a time with no worries, and therefore a respite from stress. This space refreshes and rejuvenates your body allowing it to gain the energy it needs to heal itself. You body is so grateful for this time, it will reward you by healing and continuing to be there for you.

Whenever you feel overwhelmed or trapped in pain arising from a health issue, visualize this powerful, healing, golden light enwrapping your body, sending love and energy for that part to heal. Your body knows how to realign itself into harmony, all you need to do is trust in its power and provide it the time and care it needs. Your body and I thank you for this time.

Guided Meditation for Self-healing 2

Welcome to the guided meditation for self-healing. Get yourself into a comfortable position, I recommend lying down, with earphones in so you can fully engage in your healing. The only thing you need to do is to accept healing energy, allowing it to enter every part of your body. After this meditation, let this energy remian within you, continuing to heal you for hours and even days.

So, simply allow yourself 30 minutes, where you can remain completely undisturbed.

Before this healing journey begins, let's prepare by calming yourself with some short breathing exercises. So, inhale through your nose, counting to six. One, two, three, four, five, six. Then exhale, out through your mouth, whilst counting to ten. One, two, three, four, five, six, seven, eight, nine, ten. If you find you can't reach those numbers, that's okay. Just do as your body needs.

Repeat this process again. And then, let your breathing return to its usual slow and steady rhythm. As you inhale, imagine you take in a beautiful, glistening light. Breathing out, exhale all the negativity and worries you carry with you. Notice how relaxed and lighter your body feels with every breath.

Picture yourself now, lying on a bed of soft green grass, in a beautiful garden full of colourful flowers. You lay listening to the sound of this place, the gentle chirp of insects, the soft rustling of grass in the wind and the birds as they sing. You feel peace and serenity wash over you.

Now, moving foward, we will begin to relax the entire body. Slowly take a deep breath in. Shifting your focus to your feet. Relax your toes, arch, heels, and your whole feet. Moving upwards now, relax your ankles, lower legs and knees. Enjoy the sensation as they become relaxed. Bring your focus to your thighs, the sides, front and back. Feel as they become more and more relaxed with each exhale. Now, your toes, heels and feet – relaxed. Your ankles, legs, knees and thighs- relaxed.

Place your attention to your hips, glutes, and pelvic area, now. Relax your glutes and observe how, with your every breath, your glutes and hips become looser, more relaxed and yet more free. With them the whole lower body feels the sensations relaxation brings them also.

Now, shift your awareness to your hands. Notice how you are holding them currently, and relax.

Allow your fingers to return to their natural curved position, as they do so. Relax your wrists, your forearms, your elbows, and your upper arms. Feel as your arm dangles weightlessly from your shoulders – completely relaxed.

Bring your focus to your main body, to your stomach and chest. Notice how they move easily along to the rythm of your breath. Inhale, and then relax your chest and stomach completely. Move to your lower back, noticing the surface under your back. Slowly relax your back, part by part, starting from the base of your spine, gradually moving up, all the way to the shoulders.

Enjoy the peace this moment provides. Notice how thankful your body is for recieving this calming moment. Feel how much good is happening right now!

Now, moving to the most crucial area to relax in your body, the shoulders. Here you hold the most tension, and carry the weight of most your negative thoughts and energy. So relax them, let them be loose. Observe how they become more relaxed and free with each exhale. Feel as this weight is lifted, your whole body becomes energized and refreshed, liberated from the pain and negativity holding you back.

Now, relax your neck. Relax you jaw, letting it loose. Allow your lips to sit calmly shut, your tongue resting wheres natural- completely relaxed. Relax your cheeks. Relax your eyes, your eyelids laying peacefuly over them. Relax your foreheaf. Relax the very top of your head. Now completely relaxed.

Take a deep breath, allowing the sense of peace to wash over you. Your body now completely relaxed.

Now, envision you are laying under a small, white cloud. This fluffy cloud with its idylic shape is beautiful. This cloud is here, just for you. It floats just above your head, bringing you healing power. Does it fill you with excitement? Do you feel happiness approaching?

The rain starts to drop pure droplets of light, healing rain on you. Feel these soothing drops as they fall on your face. Imagine this healing energy as small crystals, golden light or pure water, however you wish. Simply absorb and connect with its healing properties.

Feel as this healing energy beams down, enwrapping your whole head. Enjoy the sensations this energy brings. You know just what this magical cloud is doing now. It moves down to your neck. You feel as rainfrops now fall on your neck, it now becoming illumintaed with a light. Now, your head and neck are shining.

The cloud gradually makes its way down, to right above your shoulders, chest and stomach. You feel as this gentle rain touches your skin, blessing you with its healing energy. The cloud is expanding to above your arms now. Your arms and hands begin to shine as they are touched by this rain. The cloud grows, it's now above your hips, pelvis and glutes. These parts are bathed in this healing light now. Now, the cloud moves down, raindrops falling on your legs. Notice as they begin to shine themseleves. Observe the rain now, sense its purpose for you, and how it serves you. The white, healing cloud is now above you, covering your whole body, and every part in its healing raindrops. Your head is shining, your neck, shoulders, chest, stomach, arms and legs too. This rain falls on you now, a rain of light, a rain of health, and you shine brightly. Thank all this moment brings to you. You are grateful for all the healing happening right now. If you are currently facing any health issues, bring this white cloud directly on to that part, focusing its energy here. If you don't have any health issues, continue to let the rain fall over your entire body, enjoying its refreshing energy. Simply, visualize yourself shining.

This healing cloud works wonders on you. Now, you are shining brightly from its energy and your every cells brings its thanks for restoring balance in your body. Your body deserves this love and care that you have invited in now.

This time you have granted yourself, is an incredible gift to your body. Your body is thankful, and will show that in its improved performance. Enjoy this moment and your knowledge of the haeling thats occuring within your right now.

You feel comforted in every cell and every atom of your body as this light spreads through you. Any tension that remains in the body is now released, there is no longer a dark place to hide inside you. As the light rain drops fall on you, you skin may tingle or become warm. You feel all your stresses and pain, drain out of you, exactly where these drops of light have landed.

This soft light envelops you, its warm, powerful and soothing.

Enjoy the rain and all the feelings and relaxation it brings to you. Rest in it now, trusting in its work of healing you right now.

Notice as the light radiates from the center of your body. You are filled with pure, loving energy.

Now you are in this relaxed state, your body can heal itself using the infinite wisdom its recieved. As you allow this healing to take place, send yourself loving thoughts to aid this process. Utilize this moment to release the negative thinking patterns you were stuck in, that created the perfect environment for disease to flourish. This will enable you to adopt a new, healthy cycle of thinking, so you can build the perfect environment for perfect, vibrant health.

Now listen as I repeat some positive statements. Allow these ideas to enter your subconscious, allowing the growth of new positive patterns that allow health to flourish in your body and mind.

Feel free to repeat my words mentally or just simply listen to these affirmations, whilst they become your new beliefs.

I am healing my body and mind.

I am worthy of perfect health.

I forgive all I need to forgive.

I forgive myself.

I feel a growing love for myself.

I am full of life.

I take care of myself because I love myself.

I choose health for my body, mind, and spirit.

I am grateful for my amazing body and all it does every day.

I am grateful for my body and mind's health.

I am strong and powerful.

I am completely healthy to the last cell.

I am full of positive energy.

I am calm yet vibrant.

I am loved. I am enough. I am complete.

I am healing and growing.

I am letting go of everything that doesn't serve me.

I am letting go of fear, of anger, jealousy, guilt, pain and tension.

I am in peace. With no need to struggle.

I am an amazing expression of life.

I have power within me, the same power that created me.

Now, I allow that power to heal my body and mind.

The past has no power over me.

I am letting go of all now.

I am unique and wonderful.

I am worthy of love, a birthright.

I accept and appreciate myself.

I'm willing to use the energy to heal. I deserve all the best life can give. I deserve perfect health.

I am in perfect balance and in harmony with the world around me. I allow divine energy to circulate throughout my being, using its higher intelligence to heal.

Take a nice deep breath using your stomach and exhale. Notice how calm and at peace you feel. Now, whenever your ready, gently leave this meditation. Enjoy the rest of your day or, if your wish drift off into a peaceful sleep. Thank you.

Guided Meditation for Relaxation

Welcome to the meditation for reaching deep relaxation. This practice is perfect for whenever you are feeling tense or if you just simply want some time for relaxation and calmness.

Allow my voice to gently guide you to a state of deep relaxation. From there, you can easily drift off to sleep or move on with your day feeling calm and refreshed.

Find a quiet space, you can settle down in for half an hour. Get yourself into a comfortable position, sitting or lying, however you wish. Close your eyes. And allow yourself to journey into relaxation.

Take a deep breath in through your nose, and into your belly. Hold the breath for a moment, then, slowly exhale out through your mouth. Continue to do this, breathing out more slowly than your inhales, allowing your body to feel relaxed as you do so. This air works as a signal to your mind, alerting it that you are completely safe and well. So use this technique whenever you need to slow down and relax.

Breathe in. And slowly breathe out.

Repeat once more. Beathing in, and out. Now, allow your breath to return to its natural slow and steady rhythm. Just enjoy this sensation. This moment, just for you. Allow yourself to receive this care and attention. You deserve this time to be committed to simply yourself. Allow yourself to enjoy the feelings of relaxation.

Bring your attention to your breath now, how the air flows through your nose into the lungs. Feel as it moves in, expanding the walls of your chest, and then as it is released and relaxed, before your chest contracts once again.

Now, release all expectations. Remove any expectations for this meditation, don't expect certain things to occur, or an insight to come to you. Simply allow yourself to be present in this moment. You aren't needed anywhere else, but here. There is nothing you need to do now. Productiveness isn't needed right now. There is nothing else your mind needs to think about. If you find your mind does wander, bringing about random thoughts, that's okay. Just notice and acknowledge each thought briefly, before allowing it to pass. These thoughts and internal chatter will begin to fade into the background, becoming less and less noticeable. Don't engage and let these thoughts bother you. Part of your minds role is producing thoughts, and this function can't always be turned of immediatly. All you require is some time and patience, so your mind can become experianced in relaxation and having some free time to remain off duty.

Now, imagine you find yourself walking up towards the top of a hill. The day is beautiful with a clear blue sky and the sun beams down on you. The air is pleasantly warm, yet refreshingly cool. You reach the top of the hill. This place is enchanting. As you gaze into the horizon, you feel calmed by the high mountains and the winding, glittering river, down in the valley. White fluffy clouds appear sparingly in the sky, gently floating along with the soft breeze.

Now, you lie-down, onto the thick bed of green grass beneath you. It is soft and soothes your entire body. Right here, you are completely safe and free. The air from the mountains is so pure and refreshing. Take a deep breath in, allowing it to spread through your entire body. Exhale slowly.

As you lay on the soft, soothing grass, bring your focus to your body. Allow it to slip into relaxation completely. Firstly, bring attention to your toes and feet. Relax them and let them drift open slightly, up towards the sky. Feel as the grass gently tickles your feet. Now moving to your ankles, relax them. Let your calfs relax too. Move slowly upward, and relax your knees and thigh muscles. Feel the backside of your thighs, and how they feel against the grass beneath you. As you exhale, your muscles become heavier and looser. Relax your glutes, noticing again how they feel against the ground. Let your hips loosen and relax.

Your hands lay beside your body, straight and open to the sky above. Focus intentently on each finger, relaxing them one by one. Notice how they begin to softly tingle as they do so. Move to your palms now, relax them. Release all the tension you carry from your hands. Whatever you find yourself holding onto, let it go now. Simply open your palms up to the sky and allow any tension to exit. Your hands serve you all day long, they do so much for you. They deserve this relaxation. Let go of everything, from your hands. Now you feel the soft breeze on your palms. You have created a space for new energy to flow through you, energy that will serve all your true intentions. Relax your wrists and forearms. Feel the gentle touch of the grass under them now. Relax your elbows, notice how they become more loose and flexible. Release all tension from your arms and feel all the muscles in your arms as they soften.

Bring your focus your stomach. Notice how it easily expands as you inhale, just like a balloon, before contracting with your exhale. Allow your chest to relax. Feel your ribcage as it gently sits at rest.

Now it's time to relax your back. Notice how the ground feels against your back, the grass supporting it. Focus on each and every vertebrae starting from the base of your spine to your head. Take your time, making sure every single part is relaxed. Notice as the muscles in your back relax and loosen now too. Imagine your breath flowing in through your spine, before being released back out through it. Relaxing your back as you exhale.

Move to your shoulders, let them relax, loosen, and release. Notice as the softly move down from your ears, resting neutrally where's natural. Often, the weight of all the worries and stress is held on our shoulders. We aren't aware of this weight until it's released, making us feel lighter and more free.

Relax your neck and your throat. Relax the back of your head. Allow the soft green grass to support them comfortably like a pillow.

Listen to breeze as it rustles through the grass and trees. Hear the soothing song from the birds and insects in the grass. Now, allow your ears to relax. Relax your forehead and brows. Release all tension from your eyebrows and allow every tiny muscle around your eyes to relax. Calm your eyes letting them sink into your head, completely relaxed and at rest. Relax your cheeks and lips. Relax your jaw and even your tongue. Allow every part of your face to rest where is natural, rather than being held in any position.

Bring you attention to the surface of your body. Let your skin relax, visualizing how it becomes refreshed and re-energized now.

Now, focus internally. Visualize your internal organs as they relax. How every system inside you, every organ, every cell comes to rest and relax. Feel yourself internally gain fresh new energy and rejuvenate.

Your whole body is relaxed now.

Notice again how the grass feels under your body. You feel completely supported and grounded. You appreciate this grass and give it thanks for supporting and holding you now. Smile, as you enjoy this moment, the ground and the relaxation it brings to you. You thank yourself, for the gift of this moment and the care your body, mind and spirit have received. This relaxation is an invaluable gift, what your body craves most. By receiving this relaxation, your body will show its thanks by performing and serving you even better.

Right now you feel strongly grounded, yet as if your floating on the soft grass beneath you. It's time to release all the extra weight you've been carrying, any hard, dark emotions and thoughts let them go, into the ground beneath you. Imagine them as a dark sand, pouring out your body, onto the ground. Think of any worries or hard feeling you have and tell them: "I'm letting you go now. I'm devolving you to the ground. You don't serve me." Repeat this as many times as you wish, for every negative thought or emotion, and for you want to get rid of.

It's time to relax your mind now. You may find thoughts come and go. This is perfectly normal. When your relaxed, the mind notices them but lets them quickly pass by. Don't engage in them, right now is not the time to analyze these thoughts and emotions, getting caught in them. Don't follow any thought, but rather observe from a distance. Your mind is so used to working all the time, following and trusting in every thought that arises. So not engaging in them may be completely new and strange for you. Now you're at rest you can see these thoughts for what they truly are, just thoughts. These can so easily be pushed away, as they aren't truth, but simply creations of your mind.

Now, you look up at the blue sky above you. It's a perfect sunny day. The sky is almost clear, although scattered with fluffy clouds. Some of these clouds are greyish as they carry rain. You understand the meaning of these clouds - they represent your thoughts. The fluffy white clouds are your positive thoughts, the clear neutral ones are thoughts about what you need to do, where to go, the different ideas that pop up in your mind. Whereas the greyish clouds filled with rain represent your negative, difficult thoughts, worries, and fears.

You can feel a fresh breeze ripple through your hair. Although this breeze is gentle down here, up high in the sky this wind moves these clouds. The wind moves them along so each slowly disappears from view. As these clouds float away, they carry your thoughts with them. One by one, they disappear, the sky remaining a clear blue, just like your mind as it fills with clarity. Your mind is calm, resting, and you enjoy the silence of your inner mental space and the clear blue sky.

Now, you get up, standing on the soft green grass you gaze into the distance from the hill. The gentle breeze has now gained strength from the mountains around you and is now a fresh wind. It's a pleasant cold, that brings you the pure mountain air. Inhale deeply. Fill your lungs with this pure and refreshing energy. Notice if any tension and unwanted emotions remain, release them with your exhale. Whatever you don't need anymore, let it go, taken by the cleansing wind. Any tension and negativity that wasn't sent to the ground earlier, is now washed away by the wind. Any thoughts and belief that no longer serve you, let them go into the wind too. Any guilt, anger, fear, jealousy, any sour emotions, let them be taken by the wind. Floating away until they no longer remain.

The wind grows stronger now. It no longer blows gently past you, but completely through you. The wind blows through your clothes, your skin, through all your tissues and bones. All you carry that doesn't serve you, the wind takes as it flurries through you. You enjoy the sensation as the cool wind cleanses you. Allow yourself to fully experience this, trusting in the winds power and intentions. Enjoy the feeling as the pure, cool wind cleanses your entire being, leaving you feel filled with energy and clarity.

Inhale, visualizing refreshing energy fill your lungs. Exhale, releasing all mental and physical strain. It's time to get rid of any negative residue - the wind will carry it away. This time is for only you, to become reenergized and be mentally and physically cleansed, so that fresh energy, thoughts, and ideas can easily flow in.

Repeat what I say, mentally or out loud: "I inhale health."

"I breathe out," and say anything you want to release.

"I inhale prosperity."

"I breathe out," and again repeat what you want to let go.

Repeat this a few times, for everything you want to be released and cleansed by the wind.

Feel the wind flowing in and around you. Enjoy this flow and become a part of it. Simply experience this for a while.

Eventually, as the wind has cleansed all it need to, it drops back to a soft breeze. You are completely healed and cleansed now. You feel lighter, calm and energized. Your body is entirely relaxed and renewed. Your mind is fresh and clear, just like the cloudless sky.

Whenever you feel ready to leave this meditation, softly open your eyes. Return to your day and its activities, or drift off to sleep.

Whenever you are in need of being completely cleansed and reenergized, or just relaxed, you can return. The soft grass on the hill, the blue sky, the surrounding mountains, and the cleansing wind remain here for your return.

Guided Meditation for Relaxation 2

Welcome to this meditation that will assist you in reaching a deeper level of relaxation for both your body and mind.

Relaxation is a powerful tool, yet most of us don't allow ourselves the opportunity for relaxation in our usual daily lives. Often we walk through life with heavy shoulders and our bodies filled with tension. The weight of tension we carry daily can only make itself known when we relax, so often we aren't aware of how much better we can perform without it.

When we relax, so much good can happen. With regular relaxation our body can be free of any tension. Throughout our day our minds are in in constant use, so need a break once in a while to refresh. When tense, new energy and prosperity struggles to flow into our life. Through relaxation, this pathway of new energy can be opened so it can flow through us, benefiting our body and mind, in all aspects of life.

Providing yourself time for relaxation is one of the best forms of self-care. Allowing yourself this time enables you to take care of yourself, and therefore care for others too. So feel no guilt for taking the time to follow this meditation, as it is not only your highest good but also the highest good for those around you.

This time is just for you. You deserve it all. No matter what else you may need to do, allowing yourself relaxation is the best thing you can do. As this will only increase your productivity and ability to perform at your best. So, allow yourself to enjoy these precious moments.

I invite you to follow my guidance now.

Choose any place and any time of a day or night when you know you won't be disturbed. Get yourself into a comfortable position, sitting or lying down. Allow yourself to be a pleasant temperature, so use a blanket to get warm if you need.

Take a few moments to prepare for this journey by calming yourself and slowing down. Using your stomach, take a few deep breaths. As you exhale, feel your body relax more and more.

Now, imagine you are on a beautiful beach. The sun above is sowly going in, leaving a beautiful sunset. You are walk barefoot along the sand, feeling as it slinks through your toes. It's warm, soft, and feels like a gentle massage.

The warm air has a fresh seaside smell. A salty breeze brushes your face. Breathe in and let this refreshing air fill your lungs.

Now slowly breathe out.

Repeat this once again.

Inhale.

Slowly exhale.

For now, you've decided you have had enough of walking and its time to rest.

You sit or lie down on the soft sand. Now the sun is beginning to set, the sand is left with a beautiful, golden shine. It's smooth, and it shapes to support your body. You get comfortable with it, and it provides you with a soothing warmth.

You enjoy the sounds of the waves as they roll in. This is one of the most relaxing sounds in the world. The rush as the waves curl over shore, dissolving into foam.

Breathe in, deeply with your belly, and simply focus on the sounds of the waves. Release any urges to do anything, and any thoughts of your day. Right now, there is nothing else you should be doing. Just enjoy the soft touch of the sand as it supports you, how it feels under your back, legs and your hands. Notice how the warm, soothing sand cradles your head like a pillow. Breathe in with your stomach, and listen to the sounds of the sea.

Now, shift your focus to your breath. Inhale counting to four. One, two, three, four.

Hold it inside to the count of three. One, two, three.

Exhale, counting to seven. One, two, three, four, five, six, seven.

Now repeat this process again.

Inhale, counting to four. One, two, three, four.

Hold for three. One, two, three.

Exhale, for seven. One, two, three, four, five, six, seven.

Now repeat once more.

Inhale, counting to four.

Hold, counting to three.

Exhale, counting to seven.

Now, let your breathing return to its natural rhythm.

Bring your attention to your body. Notice how your body feels right now. Does it feel heavy or tense? Notice where you hold any tension in your body.

Your body does so much for you. It serves you every day in all activities and holds your beautiful soul. Take a moment to give it thanks for doing just that.

Now, we will work on relaxing the whole body, part by part.

Starting from your head, notice your forehead and eyebrows now, Inhale, as you do so scrunching them so they're tense. Exhale, allowing them to relax completely.

Now notice all the tiny muscles in your face, around your eyes, your cheek, your lips. Inhale, tensing them all. Then exhale, releasing and relaxing all these muscles too. Enjoy the rest your eyes are receiving now.

Observe any tension in the back of the head. Relax it all.

Tense your neck now. Then, count back from ten, gradually relaxing your neck and your thoat. Notice your tense shoulders and drop them down from your ears, relaxed.

Stretch your back out, so each section stands tall. With your exhale, release your back so it sits neutrally where's natural. As you slowly relax each muscle, imagine as if your whole back is recieving a calming, warm massage. Notice as you focus on each muscle, it become soothingly warm.

Take a deep breathe in, filling your lungs with refreshinga air. Breathe out, allowing your lungs to completely relax.

Bring your awareness to your abdominals. Notice how your stomach is relaxed, simply following the rhythm of your breath, epanding and contracting as you need. Feel the peace of right here.

Shift your focus to your hands. Feel the warm, soft sand beneath them. Take a moment to give thanks for your hands. For they serve you everyday, for so many years already. Stretch and extend your fingers, exhale and relax them. Relax your palms, opening them to the sky above. Tense all the muscles in your whole arm and hands now, then release them – your wrists, forearms, elbows, all the way to your shoulder.

Squeeze your glute and thighs. Exhale, release and relax. Allow them to relax your hip and pelvic area too.

Now, tense your knees and calf muscles, rasing your toes up as you do so. Allow them to tighten as much as you can, then, as you breathe out loosen them completely. Relax your whole legs now, right from your hip to your knees, and from your knees to your ankles.

Lastly, inhale tensing your feet. Then exhale, relaing them. Relax your toes, your heels, your whole foot.

Your whole body is completely relaxed now.

Enjoy the calming sensations you feel in your body right now. Feel the warm soothing rays as they set on your skin, and the soft sand that cushions your body beneath you.

Now remaining on the beach, open your eyes. You get up from the warm sand, stretching your muscles as you stand. You feel energized and refreshed.

You feel drawn to the sea, and wish to bathe in its cool, salty waters. You know this would be a wonderful healing and relaxing experiance. The sea surface sparkles under the gentle evening light. As you step into the water, imagine a golden, healing liquid enter through your feet, slowly spreading up through your legs to the rest of your body. Now your in the water neck deep, your whole body full of this glistening, golden liquid. All you don't want, any old, negative energy drains out of you, into the deep blue. This leaves room for new refreshing energy to enter within you. You dive head first into the cool water, as you do so thoughts and worries that make residence in your mind, flows out into the water. Your mind is clear and rejuvenated.

Now, you let yourself float calmly on the waters surface. You feel light and full of clarity as the sea completely supports your weight. Enjoy this deeper state of relaxation you feel right now.

When you feel ready, swim back to the beach. You return to the soft, glistening sand and wrapp yourself in a huge, soft towel. Feel its comforting warmth.

You will know when the meditation is finished, as your body and mind will feel completely relaxed, re-energized, and renewed. You will feel ready to return to your daily activities or fall asleep.

So, whenever you're ready, gently open your eyes and enjoy your day. Or, if you want, drift off to deep slumber, and have nice dreams.

Guided Meditation for Overcoming Insomnia

Welcome to the guided meditation for overcoming insomnia. If you have trouble falling asleep from time to time or seemingly everynight, this meditation is for you.

Use it in the evening before you intend to sleep. Get into your bed, and make yourself comfortable. Lie however you wish, on your back, side or stomach, whatevers most comfortable. Just listen to my voice, and allow it to guide you to a state of deep relaxation, from where you can easily drift off to sleep.

Don't worry if you fall asleep mid-way through the meditation, as my voice and guidance will still impact the subconscious mind helping you not only fall asleep easier, but also remain alseep throughout the night. I will guide you to a deeper slumber, so you will finally get a proper, productive nights rest.

Falling asleep and remaining in sleep during the whole night is a habit. Like any habit, time and practice are required for it to be formed. You can use this meditation every night, whilst you form a habit of good sleep and overcome your insomnia.

After a night of deep sleep, you will be completely rested, and be able to wake up refreshed and renewed.

You may struggle to fall asleep because you're overthinking, allowing thoughts to concern you and forming an endless to-do list. If you resonate, I would suggest pausing this right now, and writing it all down before you continue. Whatever it is, put it aside, onto paper and out your busy mind. You will deal with it tomorrow. Now, this time is for you. For relaxation, rest and to recharge.

So, shift your focus to this moment, the soft, comfortable bed you find yourself on, and to here and now. Simply relax and listen to my voice, there is nothing else you need to do. You will be guided into a perfect sleep.

Inhale deeply, and hold it to the count of three. Then, release.

Repeat this again – Inhale deeply, hold counting to three. One, two, three. Then exhale.

Now, repeat once more - breathe in, hold to the count of three. Then, breathe out.

Let your breathing drop back to its natural pattern. Don't force it into a rythm that unatural; just do what's pleasant for you.

With each exhale, let your body become lose and more relaxed.

Now, observe your thoughts as they flow by. A busy mind means your constantly preoocupied by different thoughts as they rise up like bubbles all the time. Your mind deserves a rest. Realize they are just thoughts. They are not your thoughts, but a product of a busy mind. Exhale, your mind is slowing now. Fewer and fewer thoughts arise now as your mind becomes slower and more relaxed.

Since a busy mind is used to working at all times, simply banishing thoughts entirely is not an option. But what you can do is to focus on something else. By occupying your mind with certain mindful thoughts, you can push away any unwanted ones.

So, to help keep you grounded, bring awareness to how your body feels and its physical sensations.

Become mindful of how it feels. Feel how the bed underneath you supports your bodys weight. Feel the soft, soothing warmth. Feel the weight of your bed covers, your temperature and the temperature around you. Feel the steady rhythm of your heartbeat. Listen to the sound of your breath. Feel how the cool air enters through your nose, filling your lungs. Observe how your stomach expands as you inhale.

Acknowledge any tension that exists in your body currently. Imagine it rising to the surface of your body allowing you to release it all.

Right now, there is so much in your body and surroundings that you can become aware of. Being present and mindful allows you to vacate your busy mind.

The most effective way to relax your body and mind is by placing your focus with your breath. Notice as you do so, that this also provides you with relaxing effects.

You may find completely random thoughts may arise in your mind, simply acknowledge their existance before allowing them to pass. Return your attention back to your body maintaining focus on your breath. Continue to inhale and exhale, observing how the air flows through your body and back out again.

Your breath alone will help you remain easily and naturally, calm and relaxed, so you can gradually fall asleep.

Now I invite you to use your imagination. Feel free to do so with your eyes opened or closed. It's up to you.

Visualize your mind as a spinning wheel. It spins around at a fast speed, just like your busy mind. Now, allow it to gradually slow down, more and more.

Now it's turning very slowly, it's barely moving. Time has slowed down, it's no longer something that controls you. Thoughts appear less often, they have slowed with it. You are relaxed. Your mind is calm and clear.

Your eyes begin to tire and struggle to watch the wheel as it slowly turns. They need rest. Now, push this image further and further away. It become smaller and smaller, further into your clear dark mind until it is barely even a distant dot.

Now, as you lay completly calmly you imagine you're lying under the shade of a huge tree on some soft grass. Your a shepherd and it's a lazy, warm afternoon. The evening draws nearer and you need to round up all your sheep before night falls. The sun begins to set, and you have fifty sheep to collect under the lavish orange sky. You start to count the sheep as you collect them one by one across the large field. One, two, three, four, five, six, seven, eight, nine, ten, eleven, twelve... Count further. Count until all of your sheep are safetly collected and together. You take them to their inclosure, readying them for a sleep filled night.

You are tired from your long day, so you lie on the grass once again. You're snuggling into a warm and comfortable sleeping bag. Tonight your going to sleep outdoors, accompanied by your sheep and the stars above. You gaze at the glistening stars, and think about those who will be born this very night, under these very stars. You start to give names to the stars and the children who may be born under them. The first one is Grace, and the second one is Jake, the third one is Charlie, the fourth is James, the fifth is Megan, the sixth is Rachael, the seventh is Mathew, the eighth is Helen, the ninth is Alex, the tenth is Terry... and so on. You made up ten names. Then ten more. You continue to give names to the stars and children that are going to be born until you feel so tired you struggle to think of anymore. You doze off and fall into deep, deep sleep. You will sleep the whole night undisturbed, and, when you wake in the morning, you will feel great, refreshed, and ready for a completely new day.

Guided Meditation for Overcoming Depression

Welcome to this meditation for overcoming depression.

The use of meditation for healing depression have been researched, and the techniques used in this meditation are evidence-based. So trust in this meditation whenever you are in need of relief from any sour feelings. Using this meditation daily will tremendously help you and your efforts to overcoming depression.

Your mind has become entrapped in a cycle of producing chemicals, that make you feel bad. You need to work on reversing this process, creating a habit of producing them feel-good chemicals that will make you feel great. This meditation will guide you on how to do just that. So, the goal of this meditation is to simply make you feel good. This is the soul focus of right now. Allow yourself to feel the positive effects of this meditation, you mind may show resistance to this at first, but that is because you are breaking a habit of negative thinking. With the guidance of meditation, you will build a new habit of feeling good, helping to reverse your current negative cycle of thinking. Building a new habit takes practise and time, so try to practise this meditation daily before you sleep. Enjoy the little steps you are making towards a better daily life. As you start to do small things that make you feel good, you build the foundations for a joyful, happy life.

Now, prepare yourself for relaxation. Make sure your are comfortable. Take a deep breath in and out, and relax. Simply focus on your breath right now, as we work on relaxing your entire body.

Inhale, as you do so count to four. One, two, three, four.

Exhale, counting to six while you relax your feet. One, two, three, four, five, six.

Take another deep breath, counting to four. One, two, three, four.

Release this breath, counting to six, now, relaxing your lower legs. One, two, three, four, five, six.

Inhale again, counting to four. One, two, three, four.

Exhale, until you reach six, releasing all tension from your thighs. One, two, three, four, five, six.

Take a deep breath, to the count of four.

Breathe out, relaxing your glutes, hips, and pelvic area, to the count of six.

Count to four, as you inhale.

Exhale, relaxing your fingers and palms, while you count to six.

Take another breath, to the count of four.

Breathe out, counting to six, relaxing your forearms as you do so.

Inhale deeply, until you reach the count of four.

Exhale, reaching the number six, and relaxing your elbows.

Breathe in, counting to four.

Breathe out, to the count of six, allowing the air to carry away any tension from your upper arms.

Take a breath, to the count of four, expanding your stomach.

Exhale, to the count of six, noticing how your belly contracts. Allow it to relax now.

Breathe in, counting to four.

Breathe out, to the count of six, allowing your chest to relax.

Take another deep breath, continuing to count to four.

Releasing this air, counting to six, and relaxing your whole back. Remove any hold you have over your back allowing it to sit where's natural.

Now breathe in again, to the count of four.

Breathe out, counting to six, and relaxing your shoulders. You hold lots of weight on your shoulders so repeat this once more.

Inhale, counting to four.

Exhale, to the count of six, and relax.

Breathe in - one, two, three, four.

Breathe out and relax your neck and throat - one, two, three, four, five, six.

Inhale, to the count of four.

Exhale, counting to six, and relax even the smallest muscles in your face. One, two, three, four, five, six.

You feel relaxed. Your entire body has been cleansed by the refreshing air you breathe.

Now move your attention to your mind, and the thoughts that inhabit it currently. Take a deep breath in and release, allowing them to disappear alongside your breath. Release everything that doesn't serve your true intentions. Don't be afraid to let go, you don't need these negative thoughts anymore. Let them fade away and disappear. Allow your mind to slow. Now your mind has quietened somewhat, pay attention to the thoughts that remain. Acknowledge their prescence, but continue to let your mind slow. Take a deep breath, again. Exhale, releasing your remaining thoughts with your breath again. Your mind is clear and relaxed. You feel good, completely calm and at peace. Tell yourself: I feel good and I need no reason to feel good.

Inhale deeply, Exhale. Mentally tell yourself: I feel great. But also believe it.

Breathe in and breathe out, again.

Bring your awareness to your body, noticing how it feels and any tension in it. Inhale, as you do so, allowing this tension to collect at one concentrated point inside of you. Exhale, and let it out. Release all tension along with your breath. Let it go. As you release, you start to feel even better. Breathe in and breathe out. Tell yourself again: I feel great.

Now, focus on any pain that continues to hide, deep in your body. Take a deep breath in, and exhale, releasing all that pain. You don't need pain. You are in search of feeling great. Believe it as you tell yourself: I feel great.

Do you notice any suffering in your body? It might be old self-inflicted suffering or from the present.

Whatever the suffering, bring it to the surface with your inhale. Exhale now, releasing all suffering outside, along with the breath. Let it all go. Give yourself permission to feel great.

Your body is relaxed. Your mind filled with clarity and peace. You feel great.

Notice the connection you have between your body and mind. How they work together and feel together. Truely visualize this connection. Imagine your brain as it produces chemicals that invoke feelings of happiness and joy. They feel amazing. Feel those vibrations in your mind as they make you feel wonderful in every way, and every part of you. Visualize and truely see those signals as they spread from your brain to every inch of your body.

Breathe in, and out.

Tell yourself mentally or out loud: I feel good. I feel amazing.

Your subconscious mind doesn't have the ability to distinguish between true and false. It simply believes what you tell it. So, feed your subconscious mind positivity, which will allow you to build new patterns of thinking that will work for your highest good. Feel the small pulses which begin in your brain, and travel through your whole body, spreading wonderful emotions. Enjoy these sensations and feelings your mind provides you with. Notice how the positive emotions become stronger and more prevelant as you begin to feel better and better. You deserve to feel amazing; you don't need any reasons for that. Take this time for just you, to feel great for no reason. The feelings of positivity begin to make make their pathway in your body stronger and more powerful. Allow yourself to enjoy it. Inhale. Exhale. Repeat to yourself: I feel good. I feel amazing. I am enjoying this moment.

Now, take the time to recall all you are grateful for, no matter the size and significance. Focus on all your blessings now, all that that brings you joy, all those people who bring happiness into your life, and all the joy you give to others. Feel gratitude as it spreads through you, and your subconscious, soaking it all up. Enjoy this emotion as your every cell absorbs it, remaining with it for as long as you wish. Your body and mind is filled with pure goodness right now.

As you sink into a relaxing slumber or a deep state of peace, enjoy those affirmations:

I am filled with joy.

I feel great.

Happiness fills my every cell.

I am loved.

I love myself.

I am grateful for every last blessing.

I am strong and powerful.

I am full of energy.

I see the good as it finds me.

I am complete and enough.

I deserve to feel loved and great.

My life is meaningful and I create my own purpose.

I create a better life for myself and those I love.

Gratefulness fills me.

I am thankful for all the amazing people in my life.

I am thankful for everything I encounter, and what lessons I have learned.

Thank you.

I feel amazing.

I feel valued.

Joy fills me.

Happiness fills me.

I am full of love. Love for myself, love for everything and everyone.

I am grateful.

I am full of a strong, powerful energy.

I see the good in all I encounter.

I am complete and enough.

I deserve to feel loved and great.

My life is meaningful and I create my own purpose.

I create a better life for myself and those I love.

Gratefulness fills me.

I am thankful for all the amazing people in my life.

Thank you. Thank you. Thank you.

Guided Meditation for Overcoming Depression 2

Welcome to this meditation, for escaping the cycle of depression, for those who have become entrapped by it.

People who don't understand depression and those who suffer from it, often think it is the same as being sad or unmotivated. These same people may even advise you to simply shake it off or deal with it. In reality, the truth is very different. Everyone has tough days from time to time. But, those who suffer from depression, can feel that every day is never-ending and horrid. That nothing is fulfilling anymore, and the whole world seems to have lost its colour.

In this meditation, I'll try to bring back some light and colour back into your life. We will work on noticing even the smallest positive side to all things. This may be hard, as your brain is so used to playing tricks on you. But with time, practice and consistency, you can train your mind to produce those substances that make you feel good once again. Allowing you to free yourself from a cycle of pain and negativity.

So, take a deep breath in, counting to four. One, two, three, four.

Breathe out, counting to eight. One, two, three, four, five, six, seven, eight.

Again repeat, breathing in, to four. One, two, three, four.

And breathe out, counting: one, two, three, four, five, six, seven, eight.

Now, take a deep breathe in, and hold your breath to the counting down to three - three, two, one. Breathe out, saying to yourself, "relax."

Again, breathe in, and hold - three, two, one. Exhale and "relax."

You are free to relax now; you are completely safe.

Now shift your focus to how you feel right now. Is there any tension within you? Where are you holding this tension? Notice any. It may be hiding in your neck, your shoulders, your toes, or maybe your jaw? Do you notice any emotions that fill you? Do you feel nervous, as if butterflies flutter in your stomach? Relax those parts. Take a moment to scan your whole body, start from the very top of your head, down to the tips of your toes. Notice where you hold tension in your body. Focus on those parts, allowing this tension to loosen and those parts to relax.

Perhaps your mind is filled with thoughts passing through right now. Let them all go, just as quickly as they entered. Your thoughts are just your minds doing. You don't always have to believe and follow each one. They hold no power over you, you are in control and in complete power. Just allow them to pass by, like trains as they pass a station

While we work on reversing your typical cycle of thinking, so you can see the good side of things. You mind will try to play tricks on you, as it is used to focusing solely on negativity. Time is required to rewire your brain to rewire and work properly again, so trust in the process. It is a matter of brain chemistry, but you can do a lot to ensure you gain back control, over your mind.

Now, imagine your are sat on the edge of a chair in an empty room. Your sat next to a suitcase of your stuff, and are waiting for a taxi to come and pick you up. You are ready and prepared for a journey.

Now, as you wait for a cab to come, you use this time to close your eyes and think about the different things and circumstances that have affected you recently, and what has brought you here. What does your current life look like? What has made you become seperate from your old self?

Take a moment to congratulate yourself, for truely seeing things for what they are. You have taken a huge step towards your healing and growth.

Imagine you open your eyes now. Everything makes sense now. You are filled with clarity, and can see the present clearly, without feeling the need to shift to the past and future at any point. You are aware of exactly what you need to let go. You understand that sometimes to move foward we need to let go of things first.

Your taxi is now outside, ready for you. You pick up your luggage, closing the front door behind you as you make your way to the vehicle. The driver takes your suitcases, placing them in the boot. He opens the door for you, and you're sat on the backseat. The driver starts the engine and begins to move away from the house. You look from the window, seeing your life for what it is. You observe all you don't like in your current life, it all seems greyish and tiring. You about the break you crave from it all. You know when you return your perspective will be different.

Now you have reached the train station. The kind driver smiles, and wishes you a nice holiday. You stand on the platform and await the trains arrival.

Finally the train is here. You get on and find yourself in a large carrige on your own. You take a seat and get comfortable, ready for a long ride ahead. The train departs from the station, the world outside the window looks different now. There is green all around you, beautiful green trees, fields, hills and mountains in the distance. The further you move away, the more different things look. You think about possibilities and changes. Everything can change, and there are almost limitless possibilities. Your typical plain, grey sights become green and alive. Change can be scary, but usually only brings about good things. Life is in constant change.

Now, your eyes begin to feel heavy, and you start to doze off. Feel free to take a nap if you wish. There is no where else you need to be right now, nothing else you should be doing. You have time. So rest and relax.

The train slows, and the doors open. It has arrived at the station you've been waiting for. You step off the train and find your new driver, that patiently waits for you with your name on a card. He smiles, taking you to a luxurious limousine, holding its door open for you. The seat is soft and comfortable. You feel safe. Outside, you watch as the world flows by, it's colorful and vibrant.

The taxi pulls in, into an airport for private jets. Your kind driver helps get you and your luggage onto the plane. You take a seat and make yourself comfortable, ready for your journey ahead. The pilot and a stewardess greet you with a smile. You feel welcomed and completely relaxed. The airplane leaves the ground and glides through the air. As it glides higher and higher, waves of positivity seem to flow through you more easily than before. Now, the ground disappears from sight, just like all you have left behind. You deserve this break. You sink into the chair, relaxed. Here is a comfort zone, nothing bad can happen here. So if you wish, feel free to take a nap.

The flight comes close to finishing. The plane smoothly lands. You have arrived at your destination.

Outside the airport, you look for a new taxi. You notice this place is completely different. The world from here seems so much more vibrant, colouful and the air is filled with an exciting buzz from those around you. You look foward to exploring this place further. But for now, you watch this world as it passes from the window of your taxi.

Finally, you've reached your desired destinataion. A beach stay in a small, pretty cottage. The beach your cottage looks out on is beautiful, with pearl white sand, and the sea like a melted turquoise. You step inside the cottage. Inside everything is just as relaxing and you can still hear the waves as they roll onto the beach. You take you shoes off, and head back outside. Your barefoot feels soothed by the warm soft sand and it feels relaxing to walk along the beach. It seems like such a long time ago, that you felt this relaxed. It feels like being yourself once again.

The day draws to an end, and the sun begins to set. The sky looks magnificent, it's filled with warm fiery colours, when normally it only seems to be filled with greys. You sit comfortably on the sand, and simply take in your surroundings. You notice so many things – the seagulls as they swoop up and down, the sun as it glistens on the water's surface and the water as it trickles from the rocks on the edge of the beach.

You start to feel a relaxing tired wash over you.

You make your way back to the cottage. Inside a a queen-sized bed with a comfy mattress and white sheets, waits patiently for you. You have left all your worries behind, which have been replaced with feelings of peace and serenity. You calmy lay your head down on the soft pillow and begin to fall asleep. Your muscles feel heavy and relaxed. Your mind is clear, with emotions as light as feathers, so you find it easy to drift off into a deep slumber.

When you wake, you will remember this journey and the sense of peace and tranquility it provided you with.

Guided Mindfulness Meditation for Overcoming Anxiety

Welcome to the guided meditation which uses mindfulness for overcoming anxiety. Being mindful simply means being consciously present in a moment, and aware of everything that's going on within and around you.

Today, anxiety is a common issue. Its completely unpleasant and can feel as if you are in danger at all times, although there's nothing that endangers you. Your mind does its best to try and protect you, turning on your "fight or flight,, mode preparing you for danger. Since their is no real danger this state can do more harm to you than good, so your mind is actually what endangers you most. You need to find a way to tell your mind that you are okay, that you are safe and don't need as much protection. To deliver this message to your brain, you need to calm your breathing and body, so your "fight or flight' mechanism can be switched of and your mind can slow, giving up on overprotecting you.

Often, anxiety is caused by the constant racing of our minds. Find comfort in the fact that you aren't alone in this, that many people all over the world search for ways to cope with anxiety. Fortunately you are in luck, as mindfulness can be tremendously helpful here. Since anxiety is a consequence of being mentally present in the future too much, bringing awareness to right here and now can make huge difference to you. Being mindful means you have found that golden point of awareness in the present.

Through your decision to take this time to practise this meditation, and learn more about mindfulness, means you have already taken the first step towards overcoming your anxiety.

During this meditation, our focuses will be to calm and slow the breath, becoming aware of our physical sensations, relaxing the whole body, and remaining consciously present for a while. By paying attention to our physical sensations, we can use it to ground ourselves to the present moment, heping us to stay away from the busy chaos of your mind before relaxation takes over. In turn, relaxation will remind your mind that you are in no danger and no longer needits overprotection.

So, find somewhere you can sit comfortably and quiet for the next forty minutes or so. Placing your body in comfort can put your mind at ease too. So sit or lay down, whatever you find most comfortable. Make sure your wearing loose comfortable clothing, and that you are a perfect temperature for you. Feel free to practise this meditation before sleep, simply prepare yourself for bed as you usually would.

Allow my voice to guide you through this experience, as we move towards achieving complete awareness and presence. Feel free to gently close your eyes, or keep them slightly open, either way try to stay alert for now.

Using your slight vision, or your minds eyes focus on any particular point in front of you. Narrow your focus to exactly this point, and allow everything else to fade away, simply into your surroundings.

Now, gradually allow this point of focus to grow slowly, until your whole background comes into your full field of vision. With awareness, obseve all you can see infront of you. Consciously keep your head at this exact position, and simply observe all in your view. What colours and textures can you see? Remove any judgement you may have about what you see, simply notice the colours, shapes, shades, textures and materials. Notice the tiny details that you would simply look past in everyday life.

Bring your attention to your breathing. Our breath is one of the most simple yet powerful tools for grounding ourselves in the present. Don't attempt to change anything about your breath now. Just notice its natural rythm, its depth and its natural frequency. Listen to its sound. Notice any parts of your body that move with your breath, as if connected to this air as it moves through you.

Now, with intention begin to deepen your inhale and slow down as you exhale.

Breathe in through your nose, counting to four as you do so. One, two, three, four.

Then breathe out, also through the nose, counting to six. One, two, three, four, five, six.

Repeat this process a few time more.

Inhale. One, two, three, four.

Exhale. One, two, three, four, five, six.

Breathing in this way, with exhales longer than inhales, will emphasize to your mind that you are safe to relax. That you are okay and have no need to run or fight. That you can infact rest and relax

Use this time to notice all that you can about your breath.

Pay particular attention to those perfect still moments, the pauses between every breath. Enjoy the sensation as the refreshing air fills your body, before leaving once again. Feel how it flows through you, its pathway from your nostrils, all the way to your lungs, and then back outside again.

Once again, inhale – one, two, three, four. And exhale – one, two, three, four, five, six.

If you find your regular breathing is too shallow, deeper, or you can't seem to reach those numbers, don't force it. Just try to make your exhales longer than your inhales.

As you find so often, thoughts may be flying through your mind. Don't allow these thoughts to bother you, this is perfectly normal. You mind is used to being busy, in constant worry. Just allow these thoughts to pass through, without your engagement. Imagine these thoughts and emotions as ballons in the sky, floating peacefully away. As your mind slows, fewer ballons float, their speed becoming slower and slower.

Bring your awareness to the pauses between each breath, notice your mind have similar pauses between each throught. Mentally link the two together. Allow yourself to remain in this gap between breaths and thoughts. Enjoy the peacefulness of this space, and rest here. If your mind still wanders away with these thoughts, come back to your breath and the gap between each.

Now, broaden your awareness to the physical sensations of your body.

Feel where your body connects to the surface beneath you. You may feel this line of connection is blurred, or it may feel as if a pressure or warmth. Feel your feet on this surface, or how your back feels against the chair. If you are lying, notice how the surface touches your entire back, legs and arms. Notice this surfaces temprature, its texture and what colour it feels like. Is it smooth cool, or a soft warm?

Become aware of all your senses now. Sense all you can smell. Focus on any scents you are aware of, and how they make you feel.

Then bring your attention to any sounds that surround you. What can you hear? Perhaps you can hear the gentle rumble of cars outside, the birds as they sing, or the sound of people as they go about their day. Maybe you can hear unique sounds and clicks of your house, and appliances as they're used by other members of the house. Notice the sound of your breath. Acknowledge the rhythm of your heart as it beats gently in your chest. Notice the tiniest of details in the sounds you hear. Around us, there is always so many different sounds; it's just a matter of focus if we notice them.

Begin to bring your attention to your body. Start by observing the surface of your body, your skin. Become aware of all it touches. Feel brush of your hair and clothes against it, how it lays squashed against the covers or the chair you sit on. Notice the temperature of the air that touches your skin, of this space.

Take a deep breath in, filling your stomach with calm, refreshing air. Exhale as slowly as you can, enjoying the sensation as it moves through your body.

Utilize this time, by simply being. Be aware of everything within you and around you, noticing even the smallest of details. Feel the beat of your heart and how your blood is pushed smoothly around your body.

Bring awareness to your body as a whole. Sense its aliveness in all the parts of it, in its upkeep of every system, organ and cell. Your awareness of these sensations, are the most effective tool for grounding you to the present, right now.

Inhale deeply, allowing your chest to expand thoroughly, so your stomach expands like a ballon.

As you exhale, focus on your hands, fingers, and palms. Sense the aliveness in those areas, their warmth, or slight tingling. An urge to move your fingers or hands slightly may arise, allow yourself to do so. Feel the movement, and enjoy every sensation.

Now, bring awareness to your arms. Notice everything here, your hair outside as it may rise from the cool air, or the warm flow of blood inside. Notice everything in and around your arms from your wrists to your shoulders. Feel the soft touch of the surface on the backside. Becoming so aware of a particular body part means you are completely relaxing that part.

Now shift your focus to your toes and feet. Feel any tingling in your toes, the relaxed sensation of your feet. Then allow this feeling of relaxation to spread up and through to your ankles, and then your inner legs, your knees, and upper legs. Focus on every sensation in your legs – their warmth, the point of touch between the surface and your skin. Acknowledge and enjoy the sense of relaxation in your hips, glutes, and pelvic area.

Then continue, moving your awareness up, through to your stomach and then chest. Become aware of how your stomach moves in rythm with your breathing. Feel the air as it flows through you, expanding your stomach and chestwalls, before leaving you feeling refreshed and relaxed as you exhale.

Inhale, to the count of four. One, two, three, four. Exhale, to the count of six. One, two, three, four, five, six.

Repeat this a few times more, focusing your undivided attention to how the air flows through your nose, to your lungs and stomach, before making its way back out of you.

Return your attention to the special stillness between every two breaths. Feel grounded to this space, to right now, and allow yourself to sink deeper into this pause, into peace and relaxation.

Again, if any single thought arises, just visualize it as a colorful balloon and watch as it floats peacefully away. Resist any impulse to follow it. Remain at distance from it, simply appriaciate its colour and how it smoothly drifts away from you. You are not your thoughts, they don't define you, and they have no power over you. Acknowledge them as just thoughts, a product of your mind.

Continue with your gradual scan through your body, this time moving to your back. Feel how it connects to the surface beneath or against it. The sensations your back muscles feel now. Are they loose and relaxed? Or tight and tense? Scan through your back, starting from the lowest point allowing each and every area to become relaxed. Feel where is heaviest and the most hot in your back muscles and your spine, noticing any tension that remains. Give special attention to this area, feeling as this tension slowly melts away and is released.

Now move your awareness to your neck. Feel the weight of the head it supports, and acknowledge all the sensations in your throat.

Bring your total awareness to your entire head. How often do you actually engage your focus here? Now, is the time to give it the care and attention it needs. Become aware of every sensation here. If you have hair, notice its touch on your head. Focus on each and every muscle in your face, are you holding them in a position fueled by tension? If so, let go. Scan your face with your awareness, noticing your eyes and mouth, is there any tension here? If so let go, and feel free to close your eyes now too. Take a deep breath in, and enjoy as the fresh, powerful air flows into your head. Allow this air to completely spread through you, relaxing all your muscles.

Take a few more deep breaths in. As you inhale, allow the air to bring you calmness, peace and relaxation. As you exhale, let go of all that doesn't serve your true intentions. Exhale all that tension, which prevents all the peace, clarity and joy from reaching you. As you do so, feel as your body becomes less ridgid and heavy and more soft and relaxed. Allow your body to sink into the surface beneath you, resting completely supported.

Notice all that surrounds you. Feel the temperature that runs over your skin, on your lips, your palms, your lower legs, everywhere. What sounds drift into your ears now? Take this moment to count every last thing you can hear right now. Picture how each, as they enter your ears.

Now, scan through your body once more, notice anywhere that still seems to be holding onto any tension and anxiety. Take a moment to give these areas special attention. Your body is clearly hinting at something that requires more of your time and care, and finally it will recieve just that. Sometimes, simply giving special attention to a sensation in the body is enough to loosen and remove it. So, bring your attention to these areas which are attempting to tell you something. Just stay with these sensations for a moment. You may find your mind may wander into your old patterns of thinking, if so, gently come back to this moment and stay with the experiance of these sensations.

Inhale deeply. Exhale slowly. Allow each breath to bring you peace and healing, and each exhale to take away all you need to let go.

Each moment right now, is so beneficial for you, so enjoy every last second of this time.

Just envision the healing processes that are occuring in your body right now. Feel as your organs, muscles, bones, your every system and cell is filled with a deep sense of peace and relaxation. Enjoy these feelings in your body as you allow it this time to heal and recharge. This time is for your healing alone.

Inhale calm. Exhale anxiety.

Inhale peace. Exhale tension.

Inhale relaxation. Exhale haste.

You are present and aware of all of this moment right now. This is what it feels like to be mindful. That this moment in time is your only reality. Here there is no such thing as past or future, just now. So if any worries float in your mind now, remain in this moment where they can't bother you. If these worries still bother you, imagine you are holding a big, red balloon. Open your hand, make the decision to let it go. If you still feel worries are lingering in your mind, imagine you are holding a bunch of balloons, all different sizes and colours. Then, let go, allow them all to float away from you, leaving you tied down to nothing anymore. You were the only thing holding these balloons here. You don't them anymore. Worries are just a product of your mind, attempting to keep you stuck in the past or trapped in worry over your future. You don't have to engage in them, and if you ever feel yourself drifting into these thoughts, bring your attention back to your breathing, your surroundings, and into the present.

Once you become completely aware and grounded in the present, anxiety has no place to survive. Instead it is released, away with all the colourful ballons you let go of.

Take another deep breath in again. Fill your chest with cool refreshing air, feeling as peace and calmness spreads from your stomach as you do so. Exhale, and allow every last remianing piece of anxiety, tension and business to be released.

Now listen to these affirmations, repeating them mentally or out loud and allowing them to flow through your entire being:

I am aware of my breath. I'm aware of the air as it move in and out of my body.

I am aware of my body, of its every system, of my steady hearts beat.

I am aware of my fears and anxiety. I'm aware of the pain they bring.

I am aware of the negative thoughts that produce my anxiety.

Now, I am slowing my mind.

I am calming my negative thoughts, displacing my usual anxiety.

I am relaxing my body and mind.

I am letting go of any thoughts that don't serve me. Letting go of fears and concerns.

Each moment here, I am finding more peace.

I am safe.

I am aware of my breath, and release all I don't need with my exhale.

I inhale serenity.

Everything's happening for my higher good.

Everything is in the right place.

I am divinely protected and guided.

Everything will fall into perfect place, when the time is right.

Whatever I need will find me.

Whatever I should know, is revealed to me.

I am calm and relaxed.

I am in peace with this moment, with the world, with life.

The world is a safe place for me.

I am powerful and strong.

I am present and grounded.

I am in perfect balance.

I inhale tranquility. I exhale hot tension.

As you breath, smile at yourself .

I am safe and secure. I give myself permission to be in this peace.

I am good.

Things only improve, getting better and better each day.

I anticipate great things will happen.

I accept my anxiety. It is just my mind trying to protect me. Thank you. But, I don't need you anymore. I am completely safe and well now, so I am letting you go.

Feel as you grow lighter.

I accept all of my emotions as what they are, and allow myself to experience them.

They don't define me. I can observe them whilst remaining calm.

I am healingand growing all the time.

My body and mind live together in a healthy harmony.

I allow myself to remain in peace.

I feel rejuvenated, as if reborn.

I feel wellness flow through my whole body, in each and every cell.

I am filled with a new positive energy.

I allow myself to rest in this comfort and peace.

I enjoy this soft tranquility and gentleness.

I enjoy being in this completely relaxed state, free from any anxiety.

You can start over, becoming aware of your presence as many times as you need.

In your everyday life outside meditation, look for patterns and situations where you find yourself rushing. Then, intentionally slow down, remind yourself to completely experience life fully. When we slow down, remaing with our sensations, we become aware of so much more, experiancing life fully. So, allow yourself to slow down, remain in the gap between breaths more and savour life. When you can quiet the noise in your head, you are able to see, hear and feel things with clarity, opening you up to everything around you.

Now, whenever you feel ready, gently open your eyes, stretch yourself, get up, and move on with your daily activities, try to remain slow and open to experiancing life at its fullest.

Guided Meditation For Overcoming Depression

Welcome to this meditation which aims to help in the management of depression and depressive moods.

Here, you'll engage your focus on your breath and learning how to look at your thoughts and feelings in a new way, from a new perspective.

Immediatly after this meditation you may feel more hopeful and positive, but with repeated use, you may notice feelings of depression appear less frequently. With a continued habit of mediation, you may even find yourself acting and feeling as your old self would.

This meditation can be done anywhere and anytime you wish, or whenever you may feel you need an extra boost to help manage your depression. Either way, it's best to choose a time a place you know you won't be disturbed, where you are able to close your eyes and just relax.

To begin, simply get yourself into a comfortable position. Feel free to lie down, sit on a chair or sit on the floor with your legs crossed in front of your. Its up to you, just keep your back straight and make sure your comfortabe.

Ensure your clothes are comfortable, so feel free to loosen all the restrictive pieces such as belts so you can sit softly and free. Turn off any ringers and notifications, so you won't become distracted and disturbed.

Place hands on your lap or your knees, palms facing up. If you are lying, let them straighten next to your body.

Prepare youself for relaxation, so if possible, close your eyes readying you for peace to enter.

Shift your focus to your breath. Take a few deep breaths in now. Breathe in slowly and deeply from your stomach. Connect to your breath, feeling as the cool, fresh air enters your nostrils. Notice the movement of your belly as it moves with your inhales and exhales.

Now, release any control you have over your breath, allowing it to return to its natural rhythm.

Notice every last sensation in your body. Become aware of your posture, how you hold your entire body and every part, sensing all there is to sense.

Allow your breath to flow in its natural slow and steady rhythm.

Depression is universal, a universal experiance for all humans everywhere. It affects everything - our body, the way we think and feel, all aspects of life. Depression brings along a whole host of negative thoughts and feelings that can be hard to escape from. Positivity is so much harder to find, and you may find yourself losing any interest in life. Depression can be a natural reaction to certain things life throws at you, such a loss. On the other hand, depression can seem to arise with no real cause. Either way, there is nothing wrong with you. Your thoughts and emotions are not abnormal. Although they aren't enjoyable at all, depression can actually bring you some good. It can force you to look inward, to search for solutions, reevaluate things and make adjustments, so you begin to learn more about yourself.

From time to time everyone experiances depression. But, falling into depression for too long isn't healthy. Once it has a place within you it has the ability to preserve itself, making you depressed for much longer than you should, and more and more harder to distance yourself from its hold over you.

Fortunately, once you find yourself suffering from depression, it is not a life sentence, and there is infact a solution. This meditation will teach you the techniques that help you cope with depresssion, so you can put them into practise whenever you may need them.

Firstly, you should never suppress, invalidate or ignore any emotions and thoughts. If you fight them, you only give them more power and strength, which can continue to be used against you. You also don't have to figure out the source of these thoughts and feelings, as they won't get you to the root of your problem. So, instead of attempting to force out these unlovable thoughts and emotions, it is much easier and wiser to change your relationship with them. Accept these thoughts, make a small space for them, and don't waste your energy fighting them anymore. Just by providing them this attention, you will be surprised at how easily they lose their power and fade away from you.

Bring your awareness to your body now. Ensure it is comfortable, with a neutral posture, so you can relax, yet stay alert.

Allow your breathing to remain in its natural pattern. You don't need to do anything right now, keep your breaths rhythm and depth the same. Simply breathe as you usually would. Notice the sensations in your nose now. Feel as the cool air enters your nostrils. Now, notice as the air leaves your nostrils, this time notice the airs warmth. Repeat this a few times, just focusing on the cool air as it enters and the hot, bothered air as it leaves your nostrils. Focus your complete attention on your nose now.

Repeat once more—cool air in, warm air out.

Now, fully immerse yourself in your breath and allow yourself to experience it fully. Observe your breath, be curious. Notice its every pathway around your body. Have the experience of breathing and at the same time observe yourself experiancing it.

Removing all judgement and expectations of your breath, notice your breathing's pattern. Does your breath naturally follow a long and deep rhythm? Or a short and shallow one? Notice if your breathing changes or stays the same. Don't try to change it or force it into a particular rhythm, simply leave it be, trusting your body knows best. Remove any beliefs of "how things should be." Instead, accept the things for what they are by just observing them, without trying to take control.

Continue to observe your natural pattern of breathing.

You may find at some point during the meditation, you focus starts to slip and drift off else where. This is perfectly normal, so don't get angry with yourself. We can all become distracted at times, and focusing requires practise and patience.

Distractions always come from one of three sources - your thoughts, senses, or feelings. So when you find yourself distracted, notice it, don't hold onto it and let it go. Once you've acknowledged it, return your focus back to your breath. So with your next distraction, practise this method. Notice, and let go. There is nothing you need to fight and push away, just let it float by.

Whenever your mind begins to wander, notice what's going on in the present moment. Return your focus to you nose, the sensations it feels, the cool air as you inhale and the warm air as you exhale.

You may also feel the urge to name a distraction. This could be mentally telling yourself about how the "alarm is ringing next door," how the "kids are making noise outside," the "traffic," "dog's barking," and so on, about whatever is distracting you. This is expected, but instead try to name just one thing, that's more general and more in connection with what your experiancing right now. So if you either feel your mind "distracting" or "wandering," bring your attention back to your breath. Again, try this for a moment, with the next distraction or mind wandering.

Now, the next time you lose your focus, instead of internally naming these distractions, just notice your focus has been lost and bring it right back to the present. With your next distraction practise this.

Most likely, as you struggle with depression, negative, depressive thoughts and feelings will intrude into this time. These are the thoughts you are trying to escape from the most. The trick here, is to still treat them as any other distraction. This means, rather than following them and attempting to fight them, acknowledge them for what they are and bring your attention back to your breathing. As you start to do this, it will get easier and feel more natural each time, as you already know how to let these thoughts pass. So, try it for a moment. Notice the negative thought as it appears. Gently bring your focus back to your nose and your breath. Let this thought float by easily, without any pushing.

When you seem trapped in a loop of depression and depressive thoughts, your mind is in constant focus on the future or stuck in the past. This means staying in the present, and in the sensations of your current body, helps you stay balanced. Focusing on your breathing is one of the most powerful tools for grounding you in the present, therefore helping you feel balanced. So, for the next few moments, try to remain present with your breath. Follow the airs pathway, as it enters your nostrils, filling your lungs and belly, before leaving you again. Notice even the tiniest of movements that seem to connect with your breath. Feel all the sensations this cool, refreshing air seems to provake in your body. Be intentionally present, right here, with your next few breaths.

Unfortunatly, depressive thoughts often come in hand with negative thoughts. So you may also feel distracted by feelings of sadness, emptiness, anger, frsutration, and anxiety. Emotions are a combination of thoughts and sensations in your body, which means they are often a product of depression and your minds current cycle of negativity. Acknowledge this, and begin to seperate your negative emotions into the sense in your body and the thoughts behind them. You may feel these negative emotions as an ache somewhere in your body, or a part of you that feels particulary weak and fatigued. Allow yourself to experiance all you feel, without the need to change, solve or eradicate it.

Secondly, notice the thoughts in your mind. Acknowledge the connection between these thoughts and the negative emotions you can sense in your body. Your thoughts have the ability to cause your body to feel a certain way, which is why you experaince the two together as an emotion.

Now, consciously place your attention with the sensations in your body, and not with thought. Allow your attention to rest with any sensations and notice if their instensity changes or remains the same. With your focused attention you may actually find any sensations slowly disappear.

Let emotion and the sensation stay in your body, but gentky bring your awareness back to your breath. Notice how the air flows through your body. Inhale, feel as the cool air enters your nostrils. Exhale, and focus on the warmth of the air as it leaves your nose.

When you choose to follow any distressing thoughts, it gives power to negative feelings, only making them grow stronger. In contrast, when you give your undivided attention and focus to the negative sensations they create in your body, depressive thoughts diminish, making you feel balanced and liberated from this cycle of negativity.

Feel now, as you give your breath and physical sensations your full focus, that you are completely grounded in the present, which seems to provide you with more relief than anything else.

Use this next moment to imagine you are at a train station. Around you, people rush around in all directions pushing and bumping into one another ditracted by their day and not the present moment. You stand still on the edge of the platform, awaiting your train. You notice that everything surrounding you seems grey and dull. Colourless. The faceless people who lack emotion, pace around in their grey suits. The platform itself is a dirty grey, with ugly trains that pull in every so often. You look down and see you are wearing a plain, grey almost uniform, as it lacks shape and character. You also carry a large, heavy, black bag. Your shoulder is sore from its weight, but you can't put it down. You have to carry it wherever you go.

As you stand back and observe this strange lifeless world, random thoughts may arise. If this happens, don't worry- all this mental chatter will pass. So simply acknowledge these thoughts breifly and be gentle with yourself, this is only normal. Let the people and your thoughts pass by you, they both have somewhere else they need to be. For now, you remain completely calm as you know you will be leaving this hectic yet lifeless platform soon, once your train arrives. Use this moment as a time to pause. A momentary escape from the busy world, helping you see more clearly. The train you wait for, is taking you far away, where you will feel peace and calmness. You understand you will come back changed from this journey, for the better. You are excited and ready for it to begin.

Finally, your train pulls into the station and you step aboard. You decide that this time, this journey is devoted for yourself, to simply spend time with yourself, alone with no distractions. You take a seat and begin to relax completely, you understand this trip will allow you to gain a new perspective, which you know needs to be done. So allow yourself this time, and don't feel guilty. Now your sat, you place your heavy bag down, this fills you with a deep sense of relief. Your muscles are instantly soothed and relaxed. A sense of tranquility fills both your body and mind.

Now the train moves foward, the sound of the busy rush of people at the station begins to fade away and become replaced with a peaceful quiet. You look out the window as the train glides past the same grey world. This time you can observe it from a distance, and you feel less swallowed up by its miserable chaos. Although you are leaving behind this dull world now, you may feel sadness, regret or relief, either way you know now you are leaving behind all that held you back.

Use this time for rest and relaxation. Connect with your true self and your intentions, enabling you to see your needs and desires. Any sadness you feel or negative thoughts may be trying to tell you something. Perhaps these feelings are a result of neglecting the needs of your soul. In a way to grab your attention, you unintentionally create these unpleasant feelings. Either way, you using this time to care for yourself, and relax your entire body now.

Now the train has gained some distance from your current life, you can see your life from a whole new perspective. As you look out the window, the world outside seems different. The world seems to be filled with more colour, the sky a clear blue, the trees an emerald green, not dull at all.

As you move further away from the train station, a sense of easiness grows within you, you feel at peace. You are completely relaxed and calm. Your body sinks into the comfortable chair. You arms rested from the heavy baggage you carry. Your breathing slow and steady. Your legs and feet relaxed and light. Your mind has slowed to a steady pace, filled with clarity. You feel free, in perfect balance and happy how everything seems to be working out.

Now the train stops, it has reached your destination. You pick up your large, black, heavy bag, although now it feels seemingly lighter. You walk calmly off the train, you have just a few streets to walk down, before you reach your speacil awaiting place.

The bag still seems to weigh you down slightly, but you know you can hold out until you reach your destination. You feel stronger, more powerful and determined. It will all be over soon.

Now, you stand infront of a large metal gate. With some effort, you open it and let yourself in. You are in your very own private garden. It's been quite a while since you were here last. The place looks neglected. While you have been occupied by sadness and pain, there was no one to take care of it. But now, you are ready to take care of it once more. You step on the path, that winds gently through your garden. There are no longer any flowers and grass, instead grows thick weeds and brambles. You walk towards an old tree at the back of the garden. Leaning against the trees soft bark is a large spade. You pick it up and decide to dig a large hole, in the shade of the tree. Now you have finished digging, you decide to open up your large bag. Your are curious as to what heavy baggage you have been carrying around for so long, and to your surprise you find all your worries, doubts, fears and regrets. You see them as heavy, large, grey stones. You decide its time to let go, placing them into the huge hole you have just dug. As you drop each stone into the hole one by one, name these hard feelings and mentally say to each "I'm letting you go."

So now:

Let go of sadness.

Let go of anger.

Let go of doubt.

Let go of regrets.

Let go of the pain.

Let go of hopelessness.

Let go of resentment.

Let go of bitterness.

Let go of jealousy.

Let go of hate.

Let go of misery.

Let go of helplessness.

Let go of fear.

Lct go of suffering.

Let go of uniformity.

Let go of all that makes you feel bad.

Repeat this, for as long as you need, letting go of all the stones from your bag, and finishing by burying the bag, too. Then cover the hole wil soil and feel the amazing relief.

Your eyes drift to an old bench that sits in the middle of the garden, you follow your gaze and take a seat on its warm, brown wood. As you sit here peacefully you feel at ease and completely free. Your body seems lighter, your muscles more loose. The sun above, shines down in beams through the tree's branches. Observe this garden and its current state, to fix it all and bring back its old glow, will only require a little of your energy. Giving this garden the care it deserves becomes a priority now, and you know you will enjoy the process as well as the results.

For now, just rest deeply on this bench, and imagine its final look after you have given it the care it needs. Inhale sunlight. Exhale tension. Imagine the delicate, colourful flowers. Smell the sweet roses. Feel your enthusiasm, your excitement to return the garden to a state of beauty. Realize the journey you took to get you here, was to remind you of who you really are. Smile, for your old self is back, who you really are. Simply enjoy the light as it dances around, avoiding the shadows in your garden, and mentally repeat to yourself:

I am free.

I am calm.

I am in peace.

I am grateful.

I am light.

I am happy.

I am full of love.

I am full of energy.

I am relaxed.

I am safe.

I am strong.

I am in control.

Life is good.

Life is colorful.

Life is amazing.

I love myself.

I know my worth and value.

I thankful for myself.

I accept myself.

I love life.

Now repeat these one more time:

I am free.

I am calm.

I am in peace.

I am grateful.

I am light.

I am happy.

I am full of love.

I am full of energy.

I am relaxed.

I am safe.

I am strong.

I am in control.

Life is good.

Life is colorful.

Life is amazing.

I love myself.

I know my worth and value.

I thankful for myself.

I accept myself.

I love life.

Inhale deeply and smile to yourself with your every exhale.

Just enjoy this relaxed state for a while, feeling the warm sunlight touch your skin, blessing you with its positive energy. You can take this feeling around with you as you move foward.

After you arrive home from this trip, and return to your everyday life, you will find you have been blessed with a completely new perspective.

Your private garden always waits for your return. So, don't feel a sadness as you leave, you can return whenever you wish and carry on the work with your garden.

So now, whenever your ready, gently open your eyes, returning to your day and its usual activities. Or, if you wish, keep your eyes closed and drift off into a deep, relaxing sleep.

Guided Meditation For Stress Relief

Welcome. This meditation guides you into providing you with the relief from stress you require. In today's busy world stress seems to be a common problem, that is so often looked past as normal. Generally, we don't even realize how stressed we are until we take a step back. Stress in some levels can actually be good for us, helping us stay alert and more productive, allowing us to reach certain goals and achievements. However, when stress becomes chronic, it becomes exhausting, draining all of our energy and negatively impacting all aspects of life. This is why intentionally setting aside time for stress relief and relaxation is so beneficial for you.

So feel free to use this meditation at times of particular stress, as well as the techniques we use here today. This may be before or after a stressful, tense event.

Now you are ready, find a quiet, comfortable place, where you know you won't be disturbed for the duration of this meditation. Turn off anything that could distract you, and consciously give this time solely to your well-being. You deserve this time, to simply relax and feel some relief. Naturally, are body and mind should feel at ease and relaxed. We are just taught from a young age to be stressed all the time. You body and mind need time to process our experiances, challenges, to rest, recharge and heal itself, which stress so often prevents. Now we are providing it with this time, to do all it needs.

Imagine I am here, sat with you, helping you lower your stress level, helping you feel more calm, and alleviated from the burden of stress you carry daily.

To provide you with the stress relief you need, we'll focus on three levels - your breath, your body, and your mind. The goal of which is to slow and deepen your breathing, relax your entire body and to completely calm the mind.

Understand it is okay to have thoughts that intrude your mind, this is expected during meditation, so not something you need to stress over. Allow yourself to simply remian in this moment of time. Let go of expectations and judgement you may have over this meditation, and simply enjoy all it brings to you. Just remain present here, and completely open.

Elongate your spine, allowing it to rest neutrally where is most natural. If you are sat, make sure your back is straight, yet not tensed. If your are in a lying position, make sure your spine is straight yet relaxed, as well. Either way make sure you take a comfortable, effortless position. Now prepare yourself for a deep sense of relaxation and close your eyes.

Shift your focus inward, and observe your breath. Notice its entire pathway through your body. Feel how the air effortlessly flows into your nostrils, down into your lungs and expands your stomach. Then, feel all the sensations it provides you as it leaves your stomach, then your lungs, and finally as it travels out through your nose. This process, so seemingly simple, is one of the most important connections between ourselves and life. So, notice even the tiniest of movements that connect with your breathing. In every moment there is always so much going on within our bodies, even if we may feel we are doing nothing. Notice all the sensations in the body that your breath provokes now, observing how they make you feel.

Now, let us work on deepening your breath further through the use of counting. So inhale, to the count of four. One, two, three, four.

Hold your breath as you do so, counting to three. One, two, three.

Exhale, to the count of six. One, two, three, four, five, six.

Now, repeat once more.

Inhale - one, two, three, four.

Hold - one, two, three.

Exhale - one, two, three, four, five, six.

Now, as you breathe in, visualize that you are collecting all the stress from all over your body, into a large pile. Breathe out slowly, as if you are gently blowing a dandelion. Allow this huge pile of stress, to be released with your breath.

Repeat this once again, and mentally round up all the stress and tension that remains in your body. Now, blow it all out.

Inhale, as you do so breathing in peace and tranquility. Allow these sensations to fill your stomach and lungs. Slowly exhale, mentally telling yourself: relax.

Once again, inhale deeply, taking in peace, and relaxation. Then, exhale slowly, repeating to yourself: relax.

Simply enjoy this moment, with your deep, relaxed, and slow breathing. Whenever thoughts appear, briefly notice them, before letting them pass by. Then, gently return your focus back to your breath and its pathway through your body and all the sensations this air provokes within you.

Using mindful awareness on the sensations of your body and focused attention on your breath, are effective practices for reducing stress rapidly, replacing it with feelings of relaxation. So feel free to use these techniques in everyday life, because as long as you live, your breath will always be with you, accompanying you through every challenge.

Stress in high levels has the power to interupt the body's running on so many levels. It can interfere with your blood flow, raising your blood pressure as well as your heart rhythm. It can use its influence to work on all the organs and cells of our body. Our mind also suffers, even our skin. Our brilliant bodies have the power and knowledge to heal themselves. However, when stress flows through us untamed, it becomes impossible. It's just like an organ slowly releasing poison, that we know how to heal from, but we can't compete with its continuous flow. This is why practising this meditation regularly and learning how to release stress is so tremendously beneficial.

Now, we will work on relaxing the body part by part. When your body is completely relaxed, your mind often follows, so it is important to relax the entire body. We will do this by tensing each part of the body, before allowing it to sink into complete relaxation.

So, let's start with the very bottom of your body, before working towards the very tip of our heads. Turn your awareness to your toes. Take a deep breath in and tense up the whole feet. Hold this breath and the tensed muscles in your feet and count to three. One, two, three. Now release your breath and your feet, relaxed.

With your next inhale, tense up your lower legs and knees. Hold it all there – one, two, three. And relax.

Now, take another deep breath in, this time tensing and contracting your upper legs, glutes and hips as tightly as you can. Hold- one, two, three. And release this tightness as you exhale.

Inhale, clenching your fists. Hold everything there, till three. One, two, three. Exhale slowly, releasing your grip, and allowing your fingers to spread naturally wheres comfortable. Relax your palms, letting them open up against the ceiling. Relax your wrists.

Take a deep breath in and tighten your lower arms, elbows and upper arms. Hold your breath for the next moment. One, two, three. Release all. Feel as all the muscles in your arms loosen, becoming lighter and more free.

Inhale, tensing and compressing your shoulders into your ears. Hold everything here. One, two, three, and release your breath and any tension here. Your shoulders seem less heavy and weighed down by your arms now.

With your next breath in, remain with your shoulders. Here, within our bodies we so often hold the burden of all our stress, worries and tension. So place your attention here as you hold your breath. One, two, three. Breathe out and let all the weight drop from your shoulders, completely relaxed.

Now inhale, contracting your abdominal muscles as tightly as you can as this air flows in. Pull these muscles to your spine, feeling the tension. Hold for a moment—one, two, three, and release. Let your stomach relax and allow its movements to return in synch with your breaths rhythm.

With your next breath, fill your lungs, expanding and tensing your chest. Hold as I count: one, two, three. Breathe out, releasing and relaxing your chest. Notice your ribcage now, as if its floating free, completely relaxed.

Next, move to the muscles of your back. Inhale, stretching it so it stands taller and notice all the tension in your back and spine. Hold your breath-one, two, three. Exhale, relaxing all the back muscles, one by one, so your spine is sat neutrally, straight and comfortable.

Repeat this for the neck now.

Inhale, tensing and stretching the muscles of your neck. Hold –one, two, three. Breathe out, and relax your neck. Your head seems even lighter now, your neck supporting it with ease.

With the next breath, notice the tension you feel in your scalp. Stay with these sensations for one, two, three. Breathe out and release, allowing your scalp to relax.

Now moving to your forehead, notice the intense tension in your forehead. This part often remains tense from overthinking, and never has the opportunity to relax. So breathe in, tensing it even more by raising your eyebrows. Remain here, holding this tension for- one, two, three. Then release. Now this tension finally drifts away, leaving you relaxed and calm.

Inhale, squeezing your eyes, and all the tiny eye muscles that surround them. Hold everything tight for one, two, three.Then, exhale and release all tension, allowing your eyes to relax. Now these muscles are alleviated from this tension, let your eyes sink gently into your head.

With your next breath, clench your teeth and jaw tightly together. Hold it to three. One, two, three. Breathe out and release. Allow your jaw to rest in its natural position, dropped down so your teeth don't touch. Let your tongue rest softly between, with your lips resting gently over your teeth. Your whole mouth completely releaxed.

Now we have worked through tensing and then relaxing your whole body completely. Scan through your body once more, noticing any tension that remains, clinging onto you. As you come across any tension, consciously and intentionally place relaxation there, breathing into the area and relaxing it completely.

If any stress still gathers in any corner or shadow of your body, allow it to collect on the surface. From here, the power of your breath alone can transport it away, out with your exhale.

A tense body is the result of a stressed mind. Since your body is now completely relaxed, it sends powerful signals to your mind alerting it that everything is fine, you are safe, that it can relax too. Allowing stress to drift away.

Now, your breathing is steady, deep and slow, and your body in a state of calm and relaxation, it is time for your mind to slow and become relaxed as well.

Our minds are the creater of most of our stress. It is normal to for it to produce numerous thoughts which we follow into a tangent. This means our minds become overwhelmed by the ever increasing burden of worry, fears, to-do lists and scenarios of what might or could of been. Our minds become a place of constant chaos and rush, and need the time to slow down and relax. Many health issues and conditions source, is the mind itself. So it is crucial that we learn how to soothe our minds from there heavy burdens, giving them the time to rest and recharge. Even something so powerful and wise, your brain, requires rest from time to time.

Once you accept the fact that there will always be thoughts passing through your mind, you will be able to relax on a deeper level. It is normal for these thoughts to flow by, as their production is part of the mind's role. So, don't let their presence stress you out at all.

Now, take a deep breath in. Notice the first thought that arises in your mind. Rather than engaging with it, just observe it. Then, as you breathe out, let it go.

Repeat this, with your next thought, noticing as the thought begins to form in your mind. Take a deep breath in, holding as this thought arises. Exhale, and release.

Notice how the thoughts passing through are beginning to slow, as they line up with the steady rhthym of your breath.

Although the frequency of thoughts seems to have slowed, some thoughts appear very fast, like a bouncing ball. As these appear, catch it, thowing them as far away as you can. Other thoughts arise just like big beach balls, more slowly. Some thoughts appear even slower, gently drifting over, like a balloon. Catch them briefly, and without too much force that would pop them, let them float by. As time goes on and your thoughts pass in synchrony with your breath, there will be less bouncing balls, and more slower and lighter balloons that gently float by. This means you have more control over their stay in your mind, as you should be able to gently tap them away.

You can also use this moment to imagine any harder, more heavily impacting thoughts, that result in stress, as a dark cloud. Imagine you lay under the sky. Each small dark, cloud in the sky represents a hard thought. These clouds range in colour from a light grey, to a deep black, depending on how stressful the thought behind it is.

Once every last even slightly stressful or worrying thought has been placed into the sky, you are ready to feel relief. Focus your attention onto one of these dark clouds and the stressful thought that you created it for. Inhale, and as you exhale imagine you are releasing stress. As you do this, watch this cloud as it changes colour, becoming lighter and lighter, untill its an inviting white and fluffy cloud.

Move to the next cloud now. Breathe in, and collect all your stress and darkness from the cloud. Breathe out, let go, and watch as the cloud becomes a snow white.

Inhale, moving to the next cloud, taking up all the darkness from the cloud and its thought. Exhale, breathing it all out.

Continue to do this for a while, focusing on each and every cloud until they all become a pearly white. Allow yourself to feel at ease, enjoying the escape away from your stressful thoughts. Now, they don't seem hard or dark anymore, and you feel your burden has become lighter and more easy.

Now, take a deep breath in. Exhale, and as you do so, imagine you are blowing the first white cloud away. It drifts away and slowly disappears in the distance. Where the cloud once was, is now a clear blue sky. Breathe in, repeating this process with the next cloud. Breathe out, blowing it away, leaving behind an even clearer sky.

Inhale and whilst you exhale repeat for all the rest of the clouds in your sky. Blowing them all away.

Above you is a clear, blue sky, free from any clouds. Your mind, like the sky is clear from any stressful thought. Enjoy this liberating sense of calmness, easiness, and lightness, as it spreads over you. Your mind is completely relaxed now.

Now your mind is completely calm and relaxed, return your focus to your breath.

With each breath you take, mentally repeat these affirmations to yourself:

Inhale, exhale. I am calm.

Breathe in through your nose. I am relaxed. Breathe out through your mouth.

Breathe deeply in. I feel light and at ease. Breathe out slowly.

I feel at peace.

I am confident.

I am strong.

I am focused.

Inhale and say to yourself: I can handle anything that life throws my way. Breathe out.

There is love within me.

Breathe in through your nose. I feel relaxed. Breathe out through your mouth.

I am intelligent.

I am powerful.

I am amazing.

I feel enthusiasm towards life.

Inhale. I make peace with everything inside and outside me. Exhale gently.

I enjoy the sensation as all my cells are filled with relaxation.

I bring light with me wherever I go.

I am in control and can handle everything with ease.

Breathe in through your nose. I am in perfect harmony. Breathe out.

I am calm. Breathe out.

Breathe in through your nose. I feel rejuvenated. Breathe out through your mouth.

I feel refreshed.

I feel re-energized.

I am skillful.

I am focused.

Inhale. I can handle anything that life brings me. Exhale.

I am filled with peace.

I am filled with joy.

Breathe in. Continuing to repeat these affimations to yourself.

I am relaxed. Breathe out.

I am intelligent.

I am powerful.

I am amazing.

I feel enthusiasm towards life.

Inhale. I make peace with everything outside and outside me. Exhale gently.

I enjoy the sensation as all my cells are filled with relaxation.

I bring light with me, wherever I go.

I am in control and can handle everything with ease.

Breathe in through your nose. I am in harmony. Breathe out.

Notice your body now, feeling it relaxed from head to toe. Feel the surface beneath you, completely supporting you. As you sit or lay here, imagine a cloud slowly forming underneath you. Now this cloud has grown to the size of your body, and it is the softest most comfortable thing you have ever rested on. It's supporting you perfectly, cradling and protecting your relaxed body from stress and worry, completely soft yet secure. So enjoy this moment, and simply rest on this cloud. It's here for only you.

The cloud slowly begins to drift upwards, elevating you further and further from the ground. As you float higher into the sky, you don't feel scared at all, you know you are safe here with this cloud. So enjoy this restful experiance.

Below you is the land. From high up in the sky, everything seems so small from here, and you feel comforted by how small you would look from below. You see green fields, winding rivers, old pointy mountains, you see so much. The landscape looks just like a loved, warm and colourful quilt. Now, you take a look for all those things that used to provoke your stress, from here you cant even see them! Yet these things held so much power over you. Here, on your fluffy cloud, all your troubles, worries, financial and health problems, can't bother and stress you, as they are left far down on the ground. Here, all you feel is just relaxation, peace and a feeling of ease.

Suddenly, a golden light begins to shine from the centre if your cloud. It looks just like a small sun, is shining from right behind it. The light grows stronger and stronger, so much so that the whole cloud is illuminated by this light. This light continues to grow, now moving onto your body, spreading from the points at which you touch the cloud. Your feet are now glowing, your whole legs shining. You feel as this light spreads up through to your stomach and chest, now golden. This golden light penetrates through into your arms and hands, they glow brightly too. Now your head is radiating the light too. Your whole body illuminated with this golden light. You can visably see this golden light shining from you, but you can also feel as it gently enwraps your organs and cells inside you. It fills your heart, so it now pumps this golden light around your body, just as it does blood. This light holds a healing, relaxing power, relieving you of stress. As it spreads through you, you become consumed by peace and calmness. It is everywhere, in your every cell, even your every thought. Now there is now darkness for stress to hide, so all the stress you once carried feels like a distant memory. You don't ever have to carry around so much stress, as this cloud and its golden light is never far away. For now, just bathe in this refreshing golden light, enjoying this present moment.

Now your body and mind are completely relaxed. You have drained all your stress away, and you feel liberated and free. Your breathing is deep, slow and steady, your mind filled with clarity, and your body completely relaxed. Your cloud drifts back down to the ground now. So whenever you're ready, slowly get up and depart from your cloud, ready and re-energiized.

Gently open your eyes, and return to your day, feeling completely renewed and stress-free.

Guided Meditation for Sleep-The Magic Garden (30 Minutes)

Hello and welcome to this sleep meditation. I will guide you through a journey, where you will reach deep sleep. So before we begin, get nice and comfortable in your bed. Make sure you are the perfect temperature for sleep, so not too hot or cold, as this will only occupy your busy mind later on.

To begin your journey, into a restful nights sleep we will begin by releaxing your body. When your body is completely relaxed, it sends signals to your mind telling it it is free to relax also.

So, imagine you find yourself sat or lying down on a large bench in the corner of a beautiful garden. The sun above, is starting to rise over the edges of the warm stone walls of the garden. The sun's golden light now casts your feet into brightness. This light feels soothingly warm. Inhale, allowing this powerful light to sink deep into your feet. Exhale, breathing out any tension your held there. Your feet feel calm and relaxed.

Slowly, this light spreads up, reaching your knees. You inhale deeply, allowing this light to spread deep into your lower legs, pushing away all your stresses, worries and fears away, ready to be exhaled. Now, this light has moved further into the garden, illuminating your upper legs and hips. Again, you breathe in allowing this light to completely enter. Enjoy the sensation as it spreads through you, filling your legs with its relaxing energy. Breathe out, allowing your breath to carry away any tension the light displaced.

The warm light of day continues to slowy move over your whole body, sending each part into deep relaxation. Continue to inhale, allowing this light to completely enter you, before exhaling any tension from your body. Just enjoy the sensations your body feels as it sinks deeper into relaxation. Now the light not only illuminates your body, part by part, but also the edges of the garden, hitting the plants. Like you, the plants seem to feel the powerful energy of this light, stretching and standing up taller, ready for this new day. The sun continues to rise, higher in the sky, hitting the small bushes and bouncing of the surface of the small pond in the centre of the garden.

Tonight, we will continue to explore this magical garden, allowing its enchanting powers to wash over you, relaxing you further and further, until you are ready to greet a nights restful sleep.

The sun has now moved high into the sky, so the whole garden is no longer in shadow, but in full sunlight. Your entire body is cast in this golden light. Take another deep breath, feeling as this light spreads through you, past your skin and into your every organ and system. Notice it on your forehead now, feeling its warmth, soothing your muscles, enabling you to release all tension here, so it rests completely relaxed. Infact, every last muscle in your body has been touched by this soft light, becoming more loose and light, entirely relaxed.

You look around the garden now, it seems to be wonderfully cared for, the fish in the pond healthly fed, the grass cut perfectly, no flower out of place and not a single weed in sight. The gardens beauty amazes you, for such a large space to be this perfect, it must be a miracle! You imagine you could take a pleasant stroll in this garden not matter the weather, simply because it is so wonderful.

As you sit, comfortably on the bench, notice everything there is to sense here. Listen to the sounds of the gentle breeze as it rustles through the grass and trees, notice the chirp of the crickets in the grass, and the soft song of the birds in their nests. There is so many animals that are lucky enough to call this garden home. Now, smell the potent scent of the roses as they have risen for the day. Look around at the colourful flowers, they're placment perfectly selected in rows of different colours. Just enhoy this moment, right here, in this pleasant garden.

As we move foward, through this journey of relaxation, you may find your mind wanders, bringing random thoughts and worries. If so, don't be alarmed, this is normal behaviour. Throughout your day, your mind is in constant use and may not be used to having the time to switch of and slow down. As you begin to give your mind this time to rest, it reacts by producing thoughts, with time and practise you can begin to switch of more, giving yourself the much needed time to rest, allowing you to reach a deeper, more relaxing sleep.

So, when random thoughts do arise, acknowledge their prescence briefly, rather than ignoring their existance. Then allow them to pass, bringing your focus to your breath, to this present moment, to this beautiful garden. So do this as your next thought arises. Feel the thought forming, then briefly notice it. Shift your focus back to your breath, helping to ground you in this present moment. Inhale, and exhale, allowing this thought to pass, just like the air from your body. Repeat this process with every thought, enabling you to remain in the here and now, and not distracting by any thoughts, worries or concerns.

Look around the garden once more. Part of the magic of this garden is its maintanance, there seems to be no gardener, yet it remains a utopian. This garden is open for all, yet it is so early in the day you are here alone. There is some small tasks here you decide will improve others experiance in the day. On the cobbled path, some leaves lay, blown over by the nights wind. To one side of your bench, lays a broom. You pick up the broom, walk over to the path ready to sweep the colourful leaves away. As you get nearer you notice these leaves are dark, black and crispy. Old and unwanted leaves no longer effective, just like your worries, stresses and fears, not serving your true intentions. Imagine these leaves as your darker, harder thoughts and emotions.

You begin to sweep these leaves away, beginning to clear both the path and your mind. To begin, you focus on the larger, darker and older leaves, the ones that seem to have been here a while. These leaves, are thoughts, fears, anger, guilt which you have been holding onto for too long, weighing you down. With focus and control, you sweep these leaves far away into the distance, clearing the path. Move onto the next big, dark leaf now. Again, with intention and focus you sweep this leaf away, off the path and no longer carried by you. You begin to feel lighter and your mind more clear. You continue to use your undivided focus to sweep this path clear, until no leaves remain. Your mind now liberated from these thoughts and emotions, you feel a sense of calm and peace wash over you. Remain with these sensations in your body for a moment, enjoying the sense of relaxation within you.

Now, the pathway is clear you walk over to the fountain, by the centre of the garden. The light glistens of the wild bubbly yet relaxing water, and you notice by the edge is a small net. You know what you need to do, you pick up the net, and begin to fish out the leaves from the fountain. Luckily there is not to many old leaves in the fountain, so you get to work. As you begin to clear the leaves, you look at the shiny, golden coins that rest at the bottom. There seems to be lots in the bottom, so you wonder if right now, there is something in the air, that makes peoples wishes come true. You pause for a moment, thinking about anything you would wish for. Maybe for confidence as you face a new challenge? Control over your emotions? Remaining stress free and relaxed? Whatever it may be, you think of it, as you toss a large gold coin into the fountain, that rested in your pocket all along.

Now, you return to your task of clearing the leaves from the fountain. Again each of these old leaves, represent any unpleasant thoughts. You focus on sifting these smaller leaves out of the fountain. Finally the fountain's waters seem crystal clear, not a single peice of debris float about. Like the fountain your mind is filled with clearness and clarity, no longer suffering from these thoughts you can focus on the present completely. As your mind is now, enirely relaxed.

Right now, you watch the beautiful fountain for a moment, simply taking in the majesty of the falling water. Simply enjoy the wonders of this garden completely, remaining right here, in the now. If thoughts to arise, return your focus to your breath. Feel every sensation this new refreshing air you inhale provokes. Notice how the air flows through your nose, expanding your lungs, and back out through your mouth again. Stay grounded in the present aware of the sensations of your body, feeling as you sink further into relaxation.

You turn your attention to the pond now, observing as the fish effortlessly glide through the water. As you peer over the edge of the water, the fish notice your prescence rising up to the surface, hoping you will provide them with their morning food. Searching around you notice a small tub of fish food to the right of the pond, you grab a small handful, scattering it over the water's surface. As you do so, the fish rush up to the surface in excitement, ready for their breakfast. You watch as they hoover up the food quickly, as if they've never been fed. You feel tempted to give them more, although you know you shouldn't over feed them. Instead, you turn your back on them, returning your attention to the rest of the garden.

You walk around the garden, enjoying the feeling of stillness. At this time of morning, even though no one else is around, you can still sense the activity in the garden. The feeling in the air is soothing, you are alone, but don't feel it all. The sense of flowers and trees reacting to the arrival of day fills you, filling you with their positive yet relaxing energy.

The soothing, warm energy in the garden, and the small tasks you've completed seem to have tired you. You head towards the large oak tree at the back of the garden. It is the largest oldest tree in the garden and under the shelter of its leaves seems like a pleasant place to sit and rest. You sit, leaning against its trunk, admiring its impressive size and beauty. From here you can also look out onto the whole garden, appriciating its calm, enchating allure. You feel completely relaxed and calm. This garden must truely be magic!

You sit enjoying the feelings of tranquility, peace, and harmony that fill you. Continuing to observe all this garden has to offer, and all that are lucky enough to call this garden home. Wondering about what over wishes will be made into this garden's fountain, you drift of into a restful, refreshing sleep.

Guided Meditation Returning To Sleep (30 Minutes)

Welcome to this guided meditation which will help you drift back into sleep. Waking up in the middle of the night can be very frustrating, especially if you feel wide awake and returing to sleep seems impossible. Often, this frustration is actually what prevents us sleeping once again. So, allowing yourself to slowly power down, without getting too frustrated, is important. Only once this has occured, you can return to sleep, so you can feel refreshed and ready to go in the morning.

So to begin, make sure you are ready for sleep. Lie down in bed, making yourself comfortable. Ensure you are the perfect temperature for sleep, so if your cold nestle yourself under the sheets, or remove a layer if too hot. It's important that you are able to relax both your mind and body, so maintaining the body in comfort is important as this will only distract you from sleep. Even if you are not able to drift back into sleep, just by following this meditation and relaxing the body and mind, will help you feel refreshed and energized in the morning.

So take a deep breath in, from your stomach. Then, slowly breathe out. As the air leaves your body, allow it to bring you relaxation. Take another deep breath in, exhale slowly and gently releasing any tension and frustration outside you. Now return your breathing to its natural rhythm. Allow yourself to breathe peacefully.

As you place your focus with your breath, notice how much more relaxed you have become alreday. Right now, there is nothing else you need to focus on, nothing else needs to occupy your mind. Just focus on the ins and outs of your breath. Placing your attention here, you will become more and more tired and sleepy.

Now with your next exhale, see how slowly you can release the air. Take a big, deep breath in and then slowly exhale. Very slowly and gently, see how slow you can release this breath from you. As you do this, your body can truly recognise and appriciate the relaxing sensations of your breath. Repeat this again, seeing how slowly you can exhale, before allowing your breath to return to its usual pattern.

Allow the pathway of the air you breathe, to flow through you, as it usually would. Breathe in and out without any effort and extra thought. Just trusting in your body's natural pace. Calm, soft and comfortable.

Now place your complete attention with your body. Allow your body to feel completely relaxed. Notice the stillness of your leg muscles, how heavy and warm they are. Feel how this warmth in your legs, begins to spread through your entire body. Slowly you become more and more comfortable, sinking deeper into relaxation.

Notice your shoulders as they begin to relax. Allow them to loosen and release the tension you hold there. They relax, dropping down, liberated from the weight you usually carry. Observe as your arms get heavier. This feeling of heaviness takes over your whole body and you sink deeper and deeper into your bed. Totally relaxed and comfortable.

Feel the warmth in your hands now. Appreciate this soothing sensation as this warmth spreads up into your arms, taking over your shoulders.

If your eyes are still open, notice now how they feel. Blink, observing how heavy your eyelids feel. If you desire, close your eyes, allowing your eyelids to gently rest over your eyes. Feel as your eyes sink into their sockets, completely relaxed. Now move your awareness to your forehead, notice the cool air that touches it. How smooth and relaxed it feels, free from tension.

With each exhale, imagine any feelings of tension gently flow out of you. Simply draining away, so you become more and more relaxed. Without your resistance allow this tension to drain out of you. You no longer need it.

If your mind slowly starts to drift away, don't be alarmed. Don't force anything. Just allow your mind to drift away, as if its moving down a calm beautiful river. Your focus doesn't need to remain with anything, there is nothing that needs to occupy your mind. Just embrace the feelings of calm and relaxation, allowing the feelings of tiredness enter.

As you allow your mind to move as it wishes, you will notice the tension within drift away, and become replaced with feelings of relaxation. Enjoy the feeling of soft, warmth spread through you, as you sink deeper into your bed. Let calmness and peace in. You are completely balanced and in harmony. Devoting his time for only you, and your relaxation, to rest and recharge.

Now, shift your focus back to your breath. Begin to count each and every breath. Inhaling, one. Exhaling, one. Inhaling, two. Exhaling, two. Continue to count, untill you reach five and then begin at one again. Notice as you count, you move further towards a peaceful sleep.

Continue to count your breaths. Focus on each number and the breath, in and out. If you find yourself losing count, as your mind wanders, that's okay. Just return to one and start again. Just continue counting, feeling more and more relaxed. With every number that passes, you feel more heavy, more relaxed. It becomes harder and harder to maintain your focus on the counting. You move closer to a restful, refreshing sleep.

Your mind begins to wander more, drifting further away. Drifting closer and closer to sleep. If your able to, return your mind back to the counting of your breath. Inhale, one. Exhale, one. In for two. Out for two. A sense of sleepiness washes over you, and it becomes even harder to count. For as long as possible, return your mind back to the counting.

Your body feels lighter, almost weightless like a feather. You seem to be floating in a cool breeze, yet sinking deeper into the comfort of your bed. Continue to return your mind to the counting. Inhale, one. Exhale, one. In for two. Out for two. Inhale, three. Exhale, three.

With each passing number, the sense of peace, calmness and relaxation spreads through your body further. Your body and mind, seem to greet each other in a sea of relaxation. Slowly drifting into sleep. You have no lingering frustration about your sleep being disturbed, no more thoughts to keep you awake. So, just calmly drift off, at your own pace.

Inhale, one. Exhale, one. Inhale two. Exhale, two. Inhale, three. Exhale, three.

Allow yourself to fully experience the sensation of relaxing sleep now. Your mind and body are totally free from tension and intrusive thoughts. A sense of calm has sunk deep into you as you drift off, back to sleep. You will wake in the morning, feeling completely refreshed, re-energized and ready to tackle anything your day throws at you.

Guided Meditation for sleep- The Birds Of The Mountain Forest (30 Minutes)

Hello and welcome to this journey through the mountain forest, to sleep. In this meditation we will travel through the forest, taking in all the sights and sounds, moving towards a deep state of relaxation, allowing you to drift into a deep, peaceful sleep.

So before we begin this journey, make sure you are comfortable. Lie down in your bed, get cozy under the covers so you are a perfect temperature. Discomfort will only distract you later on, so make sure you are nestled into your bed, completely comfortable. Take a deep breath in and then slowly exhale. As you breathe out, allow any tension in your body to be released. So if you are ready, let our journey begin.

Surprisingly, many peple who visit forests in the mountains often say they don't come across many signs of life. Of course all sorts of vegetation surrounds them, although they get the impression that nothing else has lived in these forests for years. Chances are though, the animals that live there have merely been scared away by the strangers presence.

To connect with all aspects of nature in the mountain forests, you have to release all tension and negative thoughts, in order for the animals to trust you. By releasing all this negative energy from within you, you can truely connect to your surroundings absorbing its positive, relaxing energy.

So to begin, turn your attention to your breathing. Take a deep breath in, feeling as the cool, refreshing air moves from your nose, into your lungs and around your body. Exhale, breathing out hot tense air. Enjoy the sensations this enchanting forest air provokes in your body, filling you with a sense of relaxation. Repeat again, inhaling slowly and deeply, filling your lungs with this magical air. Now, exhale slowly releasing any stressful, negative thoughts and emotions as you do so. Allow your breath to return to its natural rhythm, continuing to be soothed by this fresh mountain air.

Now, shift your focus to where you find yourself, in the mountain forest. Fully take in all your surroundings, the vast variety of trees, with their impressive range of sizes and shaped leaves. Some of these trees that tower over you have been here for hundreds of years. They stand tall on the mountain side provding a safe haven for a number of insects, birds and squirels. The only thing that stands any taller is the mountains themselves, that poke out of the sea of green trees.

Notice the calm feeling the forest generates, allow it to penetrate deep inside of you, into your every cell, relaxing you. As you are filled with this calming energy and you begin to become more and more relaxed, the shy animals of the forest will begin to reveal themselves to you.

You would love to see the life that calls this forest home, so let us begin to relax you body completely. You make your way towards a large oak tree and sit against its trunk. Now, we will slowly scan through your entire body, looking for any signs of tension. So to begin place your entire focus with the very top of your head and forehead. Take a deep breath in, and then exhale slowly releasing any tension here. Notice now your muscles here seem looser and more relaxed. Moving down, place your attention with every last tiny muscle in your face. Breath in, and out releasing any tension here, relaxing your face completely. If you haven't done so already, let your eyelids rest softly over your eyes, and let them sink further into your head. Continue to move down your body for the next few momoments, scanning for any signs of tension. Allow your breath to carry away, any worries and stresses that reside in your body.

(Pause for 1 minute.)

Now as you move towards the very tips of your toes, most, if not all of the tension within you has been carried away by the air you breath. Enjoy this feeling, liberated from those negative thoughts you carry around, that prevent you from reaching relaxation and fulfilling sleep.

More and more relaxed, you return you gaze to your surroundings. Above you a red squirell, stands on a branch looking down at you. It can sense you are more calm and trusts your presence, revealing itself as it stands gazing at a large nut. It takes a moment to gauge the size of this nut, wondering if it will provide him the right amount of fuel for the day, or if it will have to go foraging for more later. It briefly stares down at you, with large inviting eyes, welcoming you to the forest, before moving swiftly onwards with his prized nut.

You appreciate the trust the squirell placed with you, and it feels you with a warm calmness. Enjoy the feelings the forest provides you with now, simply remaining in this present moment. You may find your mind brings about random negative thoughts that often consume you. This is a normal reaction, for a mind not used to rest and usually in constant use, so don't be alarmed. When these thoughts arise, briefly acknowledge them before allowing them to pass, then shift your focus back to your breath, grounding you to the present moment, to the mountain forest. Practise this process, with the next thought that arises, remaining here and calm.

For now, truely experiance all this forest has to offer. As you slip deeper into relaxation, you come across more signs of life. place your undivided focus attention here, and listen to the sounds of the forest. When you first arrived, the forest was a peaceful almost silence, now you can hear the soft murmers of life. In the distance you can hear the soothing sounds of a bird's song, the rustling of squirells in the branches above and the gentle buzz of insects in the sky. These sounds send you into a deep sense of peace and relaxation.

Your mind begins to slow now, and negative thoughts that consume you so often, seem like a distant memory. Give yourself this time, and allow yourself to be soothed by the forest. You look up now and see a small blue tit attempting to strip the bark from the tree. These small birds are quite swift and are easily startled, so it here in you prescence provides you with a sense of peace. You are grateful for its company here, and the trust it places in you, as it can sense your positive thoughts and energy, that you continue to absorb from the forest.

As your mind begins to slow, and you become more and more relaxed, the forest seems to awaken more. Overhead, you notice something fly swiftly past. It seems to have gone in a flash, but you recognized it as a bald eagle. You will probably see it once again before you are ready to leave, as they tend to circle these forests, looking for food. Most of the inhabitants of the forest live among the trees, but these bald eagles are different. They make their homes high up in the mountains, so every morning they look down at their domain, in complete control of their lives.

You get up and start to move around the forest, you start to consider the size of the trees in this forest, there is no wonder why there is such an abundance of life here. You are amazed you didn't recognize all of the life here at first, and were so distracted by your negative thoughts. You stand staring at the abandunce of trees around you, that provide a home for all sorts of species of colourful, majestic birds.

The sound of bird song grows louder now, filling you with a sense of harmony and soothing your mind from its usual streem of negative thoughts. As you relax further, this song seems to sink into your every last cell, filling you with a positive energy that moves you further into relaxation. Now, you are relaxed completely, and relieved from your thoughts. You feel at peace and ready to drift of into sleep.

So, make your way towards the edge of the forest, and as you move, more and more animals seem to trust you with their presence. Their company fills you with even more peace and calmness and you are so tired you can barely move fowards. At the edge of the forest further from the taller, older trees protection, limited vegatation grows. Despite this, you see a large number of all different types of birds. They gather on the nearby braches singing a beautiful song, as if they are saying goodbye to their visitor. The wonderful chorus is so relaxing, as you drift further and further away from the forest, you can still hear it in the distance, soothing you into a peaceful, rejuvenating night's sleep. This tranquil place always awaits your return, but for now goodbye, and maybe the animals will see you again soon. Goodnight.

Guided Meditation For Sleep & Anxiety Relief (40 Minutes)

Welcome to this guided sleep meditation. One of the aims of this meditation, is to gain relief from any stress and anxiety, you suffer from daily, weighing you down. Through the use of visualisation, we will transform these negative feelings into positive feelings, so you can begin to find peace and drift off into a deep, rejuvenating night's sleep.

So to prepare yourself for this moment, for peace. Take a moment to make sure you are completely comfortable. So, lay down in your bed, get yourself into a comfortable position, the covers on or off, so you are the perfect temperature.

Now, remain in the present, becoming aware of all the sensations in your body right now. Notice the soft surface of your bed beneath you, how comfortable it feels. How you are finally settled inside its warmth, after a long, restless day. Move your attention to your mind. How does it feel right now? Is it filled with anxious thoughts that seek your attention? These thoughts may already be on your mind, but that is okay. Struggling with anxious thoughts is a normal problem, and through this meditation you will eradicate them. By relieving you of these thoughts your body and mind can have a peaceful and productive night's sleep. Remember your are worthy of just that, so let's move foward with this meditation.

So, move you focus to the sound of my voice. Those intrusive thoughts may still be trying to fight for your attention, but simply allow these thoughts to slowly drift away, and they will begin to realise that there is no space for them right now. For now, all you need to focus on is my voice. So, if you haven't done so already, feel free to close your eyes. Notice how good that feels. The warm, soothing sensation as your eyelids rest closed over your eyes, and how it slowly spreads to your forehead and up to your scalp. Although this may feel great, you can keep your eyes open for now, until they feel ready and can't resist staying open any longer.

You may find you drift off to sleep before the end of the meditation. This is okay, you will still feel the benefits of the session as your unconscious still listens to what I'm saying, impacting you even if you drift away sooner.

Remain here, in this moment, it is for you alone. Embrace all you feel, and you will begin to notice time starts to slow. Each passing moment in the present, helps you feel more and more relaxed and positive, aiding you, as you deal with those feelings of anxiety.

Now, shift your awareness to your breath. Notice how your chest gently rises and falls with every inhale and exhale. Random thoughts and feelings may continue to arise in you, if so, let them pass by before returning your attention to your breathing. Notice the natural pattern of your breath, its depth, its frequency, how it begins to slow as you become filled with feelings of peace, relaxation and calmness.

Your breathing is a constant in your life. It keeps going no matter what your conscious mind is focused on. So if ever you become distracted by negative, hard thoughts use it to ground you to the present moment. Fully experiance your breath now, with your full concentration. This may feel strange if you have never done this before. These sensations you feel right now, are occuring within you in the present moment, and you aren't distracted by thoughts on the past of future, but with right now. As you focus completely on your breath now, enjoy the feelings of peace your mind recieves and deserves.

With every exhale you become more relaxed, moving into a complete state of peace. Notice the changes that have occured within you already. You feel more comfortable, tension seems to be slipping away, soothed by your breath. You are amazed that simply by focusing on your breathing, you have been able to slip into a wonderful, tranquil place of peace.

Now, take longer breaths. Inhale slowly and gently, and exhale for much longer than you usually would. As you breath in this rhythm, notice how your body seems to slip further into relaxation. Observe the rise and fall of your chest, how your stomach moves in connection with your breath too. Take a deep breath in, feeling as your chest and stomach rise. Then, breathe out, noticing as the muscles in your chest gradually relax and lower again. Enjoy this process, and the sensations the air provokes within you.

Allow your breath to return to its regular pattern. Experiance what it is like to have full control over your breath, as you begin to expand your awareness. Become aware of all your body feels, right from the very top of your head to the tips of your toes. As you do so, notice any tension you feel and where it resides within you. Take the next few moments to just notice any tension, and how it makes you feel.

Using the power of your imagination, visualize a large selection of candles in front of you. Each one represents a piece of tension within you. They flicker softly, attempting to grab you attention. So, take a quick moment to observe these candles prescence.

Now place your attention with one of the large candles as well as the tension it represents. Using your undivided attention here, take a deep breath in. Hold this breath inside you, allowing this refreshing air to move towards this tension. Exhale, allowing this tension to slowly drift away, blowing out that candle. The tension in that area seems to have slowly drained away, leaving you feeling relief. Now, turn to another candle. Place your focus with it and the tension it represents, and inhale. Then exhale, noticing this candle is now blown out.

As you continue to work on each candle, you release the stresses and tensions that were fueling your anxiety. By doing so, you provide your body and mind the space it requires to rest and recharge. As you cleanse your mind from these negative thoughts, you give it more space to be filled with positive thoughts and emotions. So allow yourself this time to rest and recharge, allowing you to enter sleep liberated from your pattern of negative thinking and stresses.

Move foward, continuing to blow out the candles one by one. Notice how you feel as you blow out each one, as you move closer to a peaceful night's sleep. You are so close to releasing all tension from your body, replacing it with positive energy.

Now, as you have less and less candles to blow out, notice how your body and mind communicate. Notice every signal between them, how these connections are beginning to blur. Now your body and mind, and the line between each is unclear, seemingly becoming one. They feel as if they are one entity, where you can truely sense all the different sensations relaxation brings. This feeling only greatens with each candle you blow out. Now your mind feels free, there is nothing stopping you fully experiancing the sense of calmness you feel. Another candle blown out, a stop towards complete balance, a step towards perfect rest.

Now just one candle remains lit. With one long exhalation blow it out. You feel completely liberated from stress, tension and anxiety. Now if you have room, stretch yourself out a little, making yourself as long as possible. Place your awareness with your breath, noticing how much it has slowed now. With every breath, you are becoming more relaxed.

Now you feel relaxed and peaceful, your mind may wander bringing up what gave you stress and anxiety today. Just observe these thoughts, these feelings are completely valid and aren't something you have to completely push away. Don't let these thoughts eat into your conscious mind, but let them briefly pass. If these thoughts becoming too distracting, and you begin to engage in them, bring your mind back to your breathing, to the present moment, where you are completely relaxed.

Any anxious feelings, stressed emotions and recurring negative thoughts that remain, imagine them as balloons. Let them drift away, floating peacefully as a balloon would in the vast sky. Imagine these thoughts and emotions drifting away from you and your bed, enjoying the sensations this brings you. Notice the relief you feel, your body and mind seem lighter and more free now.

Now these anxious thoughts and feelings have drifted far away, completely gone. No longer inn view, as if they never even existed. Now, you don't need to worry about anxiety having so much of an effect over you. You know that if it ever begins to gain control over you again, giving yourself some time and space like you are right now, will give you the relief you deserve.

Just allow yourself to appreciate the calm, serenity of right now. This feeling is like no other you experiance in daily life, and you have created it from the power of your mind alone. If it ever seems that anxiety has taken control over you, keeping you awake at night, feel relief that you can always return to this meditation, where you can release all these negative feelings. This experiance and the relaxing peace it brings to you, is always here if you need.

The only thing you need to do is provide yourself the time and space you deserve, so you can feel rejuvenated and refreshed.

Now, we will begin to count down from five to one. With each number we count, you will sink deeper into a state of complete relaxation. Once we reach the number one, you will have drifted off, into a peaceful, refreshing night's sleep, where you will wake refreshed and confident in your abilitites tomorrow morning.

Five. Place your focus with your breath. Fully experience the sensation of your regular pattern of breathing. How with every exhale, tension is carried away from your body. How when your completely connected with breathing you reach another level of peace.

Four. Allow relaxation to take over. Grant yourself this moment, to experiance relaxation alone. Rember all the candles you blew out earlier, and all the tension you blew away. You don't need those feelings of worry and anxiety anymore, so let them stay away. Just focus on yourself and your journey into a deeper sense of relaxation.

Three. Your eyes should be closed now, enjoy the sensation as your eyes are soothed with this relaxing rest. Sink deeper into your bed. Conscious thoughts, like your worries should have drifted away now.

Your focus should be alone with the sensations of your body and mind now. Allow other thoughts to float away from you, this is not the time to focus on them.

Two, sink deeper still. Every last muscle within you, feels warm and heavy, feel as they sink deeper into the comfort of your bed. Embrace all it feels like to be completely centred, totally at peace, free from negativity. Your body and mind are free, working together in unision.

One. Drift further into relaxation. Sense wonderful feelings of positivity and harmony, as they wash over you, absorbed by your every last cell. You start to drift into sleep, knowing you deserve this time for rest, recovery and peace.

Drifting off to sleep now, you become fully prepared for tomorrow. You will be able to embrace all the day has to offer, knowing you have complete control over your mind and emotions. This meditation can always be completed again, whenever you feel overwhelmed, struggling to settle into a restful, productive night's sleep. You know you deserve this time to rest, so sink deeper into your bed, enjoying its comfort and slowly drift away, into sleep.